THE
SALAMANCA
CAMPAIGN
1812

CAPTAIN A. H. MARINDIN
The Black Watch

The Naval & Military Press Ltd

Published by
The Naval & Military Press Ltd
Unit 10 Ridgewood Industrial Park,
Uckfield, East Sussex,
TN22 5QE England
Tel: +44 (0) 1825 749494
Fax: +44 (0) 1825 765701
www.naval-military-press.com

The Naval & Military
Press

MILITARY HISTORY AT YOUR
FINGERTIPS

... a unique and expanding series of reference works

Working in collaboration with the foremost
regiments and institutions, as well as acknowledged
experts in their field, N&MP have assembled a
formidable array of titles including technologically
advanced CD-ROMs and facsimile reprints of
impossible-to-find rarities.

PREFACE.

IN putting forward this short account of the Salamanca Campaign, I make no attempt at producing a readable or popular narrative of the events of 1812.

My intention is to sift out the facts, as described by the various authorities, and to clear the ground, as far as possible, of debatable matter, so that the student of the Campaign may have a framework which he can fill in from the glowing narratives of Napier, Thiers, Alison, and others, and on which he can build his conclusions as to the lessons which may be useful in future wars.

The object of studying Military History is to deduce lessons which may be useful in the future, and to do for the soldier what 'friendly games' or 'trial eights' do for the football team or rowing men, entered for important events.

But, too often, the student of a campaign becomes so involved in matters of detail—*e.g.*, as to whether there were 108 or 102 guns at a certain point, or whether it was X.'s brigade or Y.'s brigade that led at a certain critical moment—that he neglects the lessons which may be useful in the future, and becomes entangled in a mass of argument on subjects that, from a practical point of view, matter very little.

This account, therefore, of the events of 1812 is intended to clear the way, so that the student may devote his whole attention to deducing the lessons of the campaign.

The Salamanca Campaign is peculiarly interesting as a military study, because 'Greek met Greek.' It was not one-sided in any way.

The Austerlitz or Jena Campaigns are deeply interesting studies, but in both cases there was a master-mind on one side.

PREFACE.

In the Franco-German War the organization and strategical conceptions on the one side were so overwhelmingly superior that the other side, in spite of its gallant fighting and tactical leading, had little chance of winning.

In this campaign two good men met, and, on the eve of the final scene, the eventual victor was 'deeply disquieted.'

At the end of this book certain lessons are alluded to and certain deductions drawn. The student may agree with them or he may not. In the latter case—since to disagree often shows more active interest than to agree—good will result, provided the campaign has been studied as a kind of mental military gymnastics with a view to training the mind to think out the lessons which may be useful in the future.

Those who are within reach of the United Service Institution in London, or the U.S.I. in Simla, or of any other good Military Library, should read through the Despatches and Orders relating to this Campaign in Vol. IX., *Wellington's Despatches* (Gurwood), and Vols. VII. and XIV., *Wellington's Supplementary Despatches.*

There are few finer examples of an 'appreciation of the situation' than those contained in Wellington's despatches to Lord Liverpool on May 26th and June 18th, and to Earl Bathurst on July 21st, and there is no more straightforward or simple account of the operations on the Allied side than that recorded in these letters and despatches.

The detailed movements of the French on July 22nd, discussed in the Appendix, are very difficult to describe accurately, and I shall be very grateful to any one who will supply me, through the publishers, with any authentic information or maps which will enable me to solve this question in a future edition.

CONTENTS.

CONTENTS.

CHAPTER V.

Battle of Salamanca, July 22nd.

	PAGE
PRELIMINARY OBSERVATIONS	27–28
ORDRE DE BATAILLE ON BOTH SIDES	29
NOTE ON HISTORICAL ACCURACY	30
PRELIMINARY MOVES ON THE MORNING OF THE 22ND	30
WELLINGTON'S PRELIMINARY DISPOSITIONS	31
MARMONT'S DISPOSITIONS—GAP IN THE FRENCH LINE	31–32
WELLINGTON'S NEW DISPOSITIONS	33
THE BATTLE	34–36
FRENCH REARGUARD AND WELLINGTON'S DISPOSITIONS FOR DRIVING IT IN	36
PURSUIT	37
LOSSES	38

CHAPTER VI.

NOTES—DISCUSSION OF CRITICISMS—LESSONS AND POINTS TO BE THOUGHT OUT	39–49

————

WELLINGTON'S GENERAL ORDER TO THE TROOPS AFTER SALAMANCA	50

————

APPENDIX.

DISCUSSION AS TO THE NAMES OF THE FRENCH COMMANDERS WHO LED THE EXTENSION TO THE LEFT	51–53
EXTRACTS FROM VARIOUS AUTHORITIES	54–59

LIST OF AUTHORITIES CONSULTED.

1. 'Encyclopædia Britannica.'
2. 'Wellington's Despatches' (Gurwood).   Vol. IX.
3. 'Wellington's Supplementary Despatches.'   Vols. VII. and XIV.
4. Marmont—'Mémoires et Correspondance.'   Vol. IV.
5. Napier—'History of the Peninsular War.'   Vol. IV.
6.   „   „   „   „   „   Translation & Notes—Dumas.
7. Jones—'Account of the War in Spain and France.'
8. Alison—'History of Europe.'   Vol. X.   (See especially edition of 1860.)
9. Hamley—'Operations of War.'
10. Thiers—'Histoire du Consulat et de l'Empire.'   Vol. XV.
11. Jomini—
12. Kausler—'Atlas des plus mémorables batailles.'
13. Gleig—'Life of Wellington.'   Translated by Gleig.
14. Maxwell—'Life of Wellington.'
15. Morris—'Great Commanders of Modern Times.'
16.   —'Histoire de la Guerre de la Peninsule.'
17. Butler—'Wellington's Operations in the Peninsula.'
18. 'Victoires, conquêtes et guerres des Français.'   Vol. II.
19. 'Memoirs of Sir Thomas Picton.'
20. 'Napoleon as a General.'
21. Vial.
22. Adams.
23. Derrécagaix.
24. Blume.
25. Hohenlohe Letters.

These give little information about this campaign, and are only mentioned here to save the student from wasting time by searching through them.

MAPS.

1. Alison's 'History of Europe.'   Atlas.
2. 'Geological Survey of Spain.'
3. 'Carte par Chef de Bat. J. M. Carvallo, pour' No. 16, above.
4. Kausler's Atlas.
5. Large Map of the Battlefield.   By Major Mitchell.

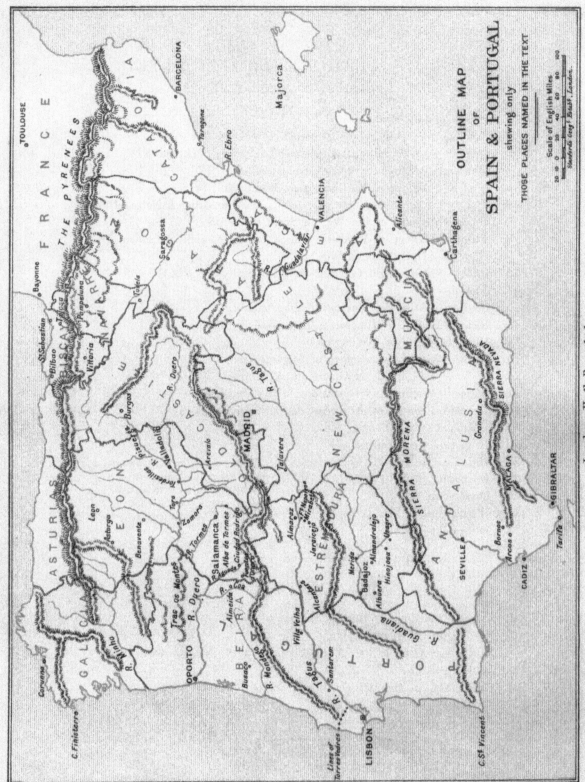

OUTLINE MAP
OF
SPAIN & PORTUGAL
shewing only
THOSE PLACES NAMED IN THE TEXT

Scale of English Miles.
20 10 0 20 40 60 80 100

Stanford's Geog'. Estab'. London.

London : Hugh Rees, Ltd.

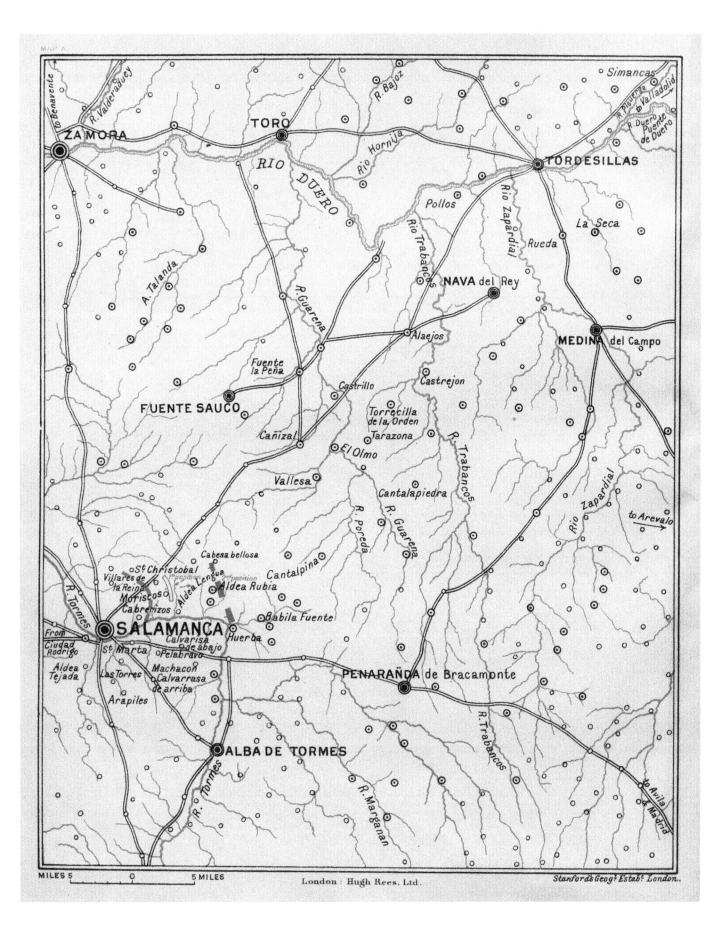

MILES 5   5 MILES

Stanford's Geog.l Estab.t London.

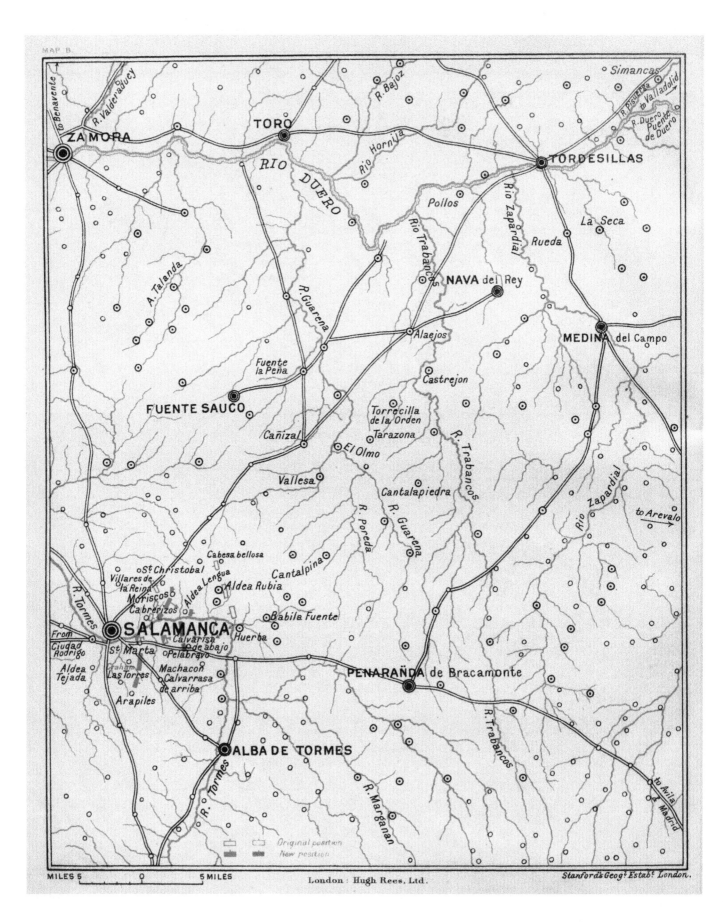

MAP B.

to Benavente

R. Valderaduey

ZAMORA

TORO

RIO DUERO

R. Bajoz

R. Pisuerga
to Valladolid
Simancas
R. Duero
Puente
de Duero

TORDESILLAS

Rio Hornija

Pollos

Rio Zapardial

La Seca

Rio Trabancos

Rueda

A. Talanda

NAVA del Rey

R. Guarena

MEDINA del Campo

Fuente
la Peña

Alaejos

Castrejon

FUENTE SAUCO

Torrecilla
de la Orden

Cañizal

Tarazona

R. Trabancos

El Olmo

Vallesa

Cantalapiedra

Rio Zapardial

R. Poveda

R. Guarena

to Arevalo

Cabesa bellosa

oSt Christobal

Cantalpina

Villares de
la Reina

Aldea Lengua

Aldea Rubia

Moriscos

Cabrerizos

Babila Fuente

From
Ciudad
Rodrigo

SALAMANCA

St Marta

Calvarisa
de abajo
oPelabravo

Huerba

R. Tormes

Aldea
Tejada

Graham

Las Torres

Machacon
Calvarrasa
de arriba

PEÑARANDA de Bracamonte

Arapiles

R. Trabancos

ALBA DE TORMES

to Avila
Madrid

R. Tormes

R. Marganan

Original position
New position

MILES 5   0   5 MILES

London : Hugh Rees, Ltd.

Stanford's Geog.l Estab.t London.

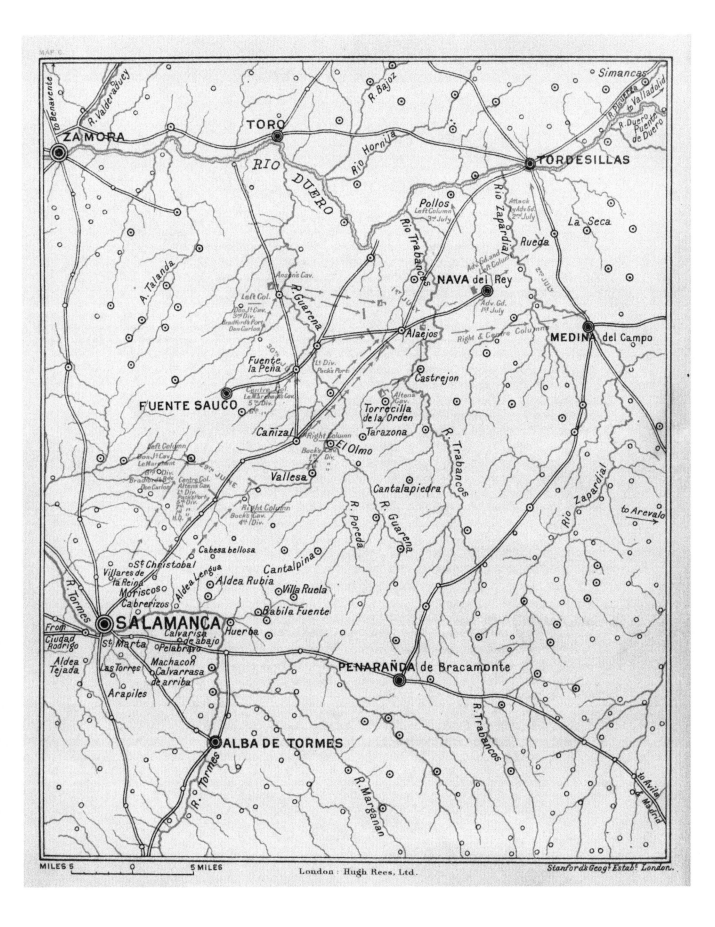

MAP C

ZAMORA

to Benavente

R. Valderaduey

TORO

RIO DUERO

Rio Hornija

R. Bajoz

Simancas

TORDESILLAS

R. Pisuerga
to Valladolid

R. Duero
Puente
de Duero

Pollos
Left Column
3rd July

Rio Zapardiel

Attack
by Adv. Gd.
2nd July

La Seca

Rueda

2nd JULY

Rio Trabancos

NAVA del Rey

Adv. Gd. and
Left Colum

A. Talanda

Anson's Cav.

R. Guarena

Left Col.
Don 1st Cav.
3rd Div.
Bradford's Port.
Don Carlos

1st JULY

Alaejos

Adv. Gd.
1st July

MEDINA del Campo

Right & Centre Column

Castrejon

Fuente
la Pena

Lt. Div.
Pack's Port.

FUENTE SAUCO

Centre Col.
Le Marchant's Cav.
5th Div.
3rd

30th

Altens
Cav.

Torrecilla
de la Orden

Canizal

Right Column
Pack's
Cav.
Div.

El Olmo

Tarazona

R. Trabancos

Left Column
Don 1st Cav.
Le Marchant
8th Div.
Bradford 8th
Don Carlos

29th JUNE

Centre Col.
Altens Cav.
Lt. Div. Port.
5th Div.
7th
H.Q.

Vallesa

Right Column
Pack's Cav.
4th Div.

Cantalapiedra

R. Poreda

R. Guarena

Rio Zapardial

to Arevalo

Cabesa bellosa

Cantalpina

St. Christobal

Villares de
la Reina

Aldea Lengua

Aldea Rubia

Moriscos

Cabrerizos

Villa Ruela

Babila Fuente

R. Tormes

SALAMANCA

Huerba

From
Ciudad
Rodrigo

St. Marta

Calvarisa
de abajo

Pelabravo

PENARANDA de Bracamonte

Aldea
Tejada

Las Torres

Machacon
Calvarrasa
de arriba

R. Trabancos

Arapiles

ALBA DE TORMES

R. Tormes

R. Marganan

to Avila
& Madrid

MILES 5   0   5 MILES

London: Hugh Rees, Ltd.

Stanford's Geog.l Estab.t London.

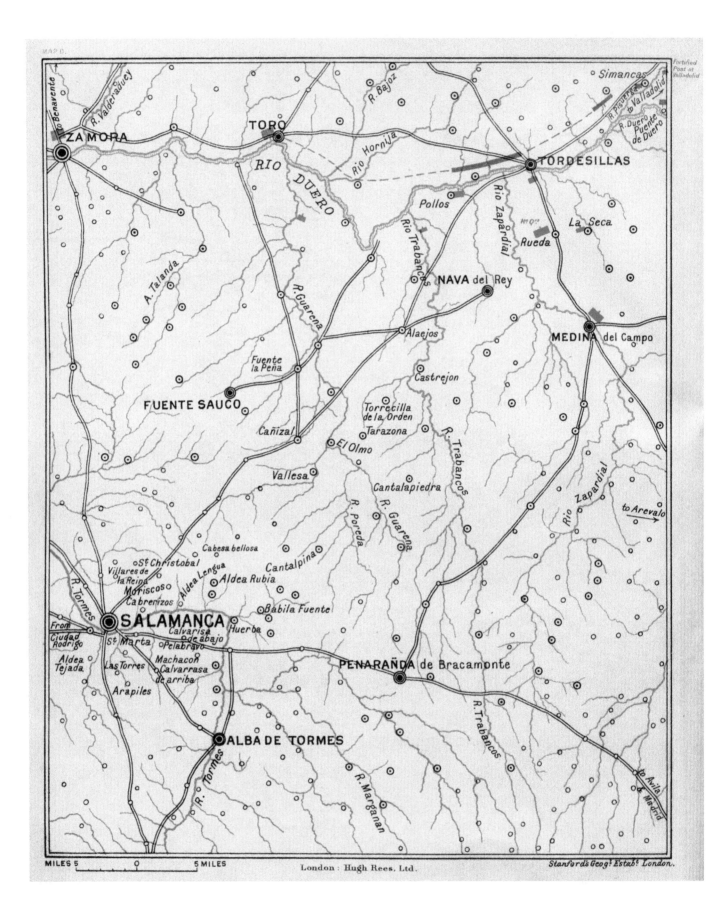

MAP 0.

Fortified
Post at
Valladolid

Simancas

R. Pisuerga
to Valladolid

R. Duero
Puente
de Duero

R.º Benavente

R. Valderaduey

R. Bajoz

ZAMORA

TORO

RIO DUERO

Rio Hornija

TORDESILLAS

Pollos

Rio Zapardial

La Seca

H.º Q.º

Rueda

A. Talanda

Rio Trabancos

R. Guarena

NAVA del Rey

MEDINA del Campo

Alaejos

Fuente
la Peña

Castrejon

FUENTE SAUCO

Torrecilla
de la Orden

Cañizal

Tarazona

R. Trabancos

El Olmo

Vallesa

Cantalapiedra

Rio Zapardial

R. Guarena

R. Poveda

to Arevalo

Cabesa bellosa

Cantalpina

St Christobal

Villares de
la Reina

Aldea Lengua

Aldea Rubia

Moriscos

Cabrerizos

R. Tormes

Babila Fuente

From
Ciudad
Rodrigo

SALAMANCA

Calvarisa
de abajo

Huerba

St Marta

Pelabravo

Aldea
Tejada

Machacon
Calvarrasa
de arriba

Las Torres

PENARANDA de Bracamonte

Arapiles

R. Trabancos

ALBA DE TORMES

R. Tormes

R. Marganan

to Avila
& Madrid

MILES 5   0   5 MILES

London : Hugh Rees, Ltd.

Stanford's Geog.ᶩ Estab.ᵗ London.

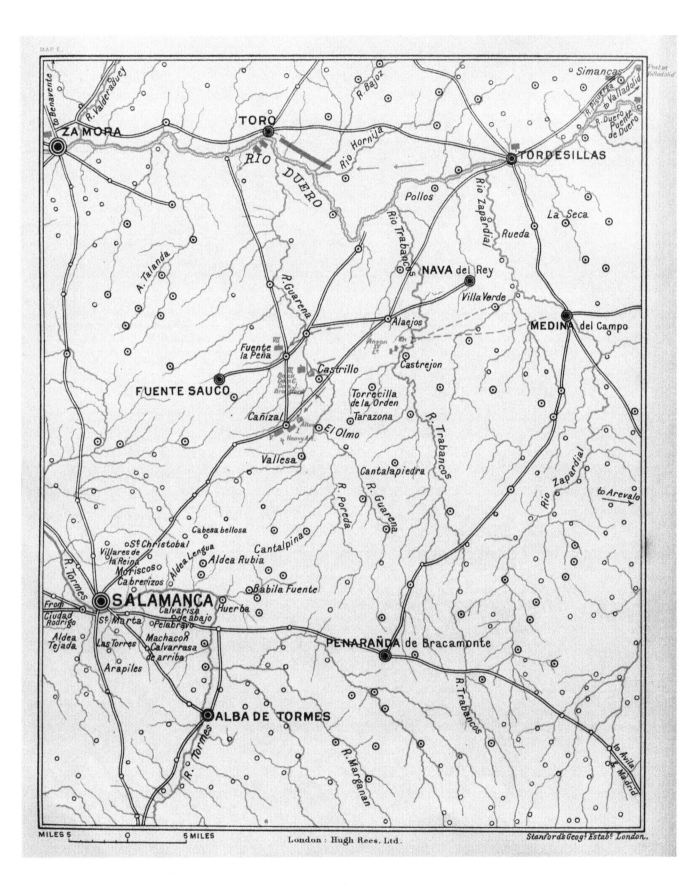

MAP E.

Simancas   *Post at Valladolid*

R. Pisuerga
to Valladolid
R. Duero
Puente de Duero

ZAMORA

to Benavente

R. Valderaduey

TORO

R. Bajoz

Rio Hornija

TORDESILLAS

RIO

DUERO

Pollos

Rio Zapardial

La Seca

Rueda

A. Talanda

R. Guarena

Rio Trabancos

NAVA del Rey

Villa Verde

MEDINA del Campo

Alaejos

Anson
IV
Lt

Fuente la Peña

III

Castrillo

Castrejon

FUENTE SAUCO

Back
Def
Bradford

Cañizal

Alten
I
Heavy Art

El Olmo

Torrecilla de la Orden

Tarazona

R. Trabancos

Vallesa

Cantalapiedra

R. Poreda

R. Trabancos

R. Guarena

Rio Zapardial

to Arevalo

Cabesa bellosa

Cantalpina

St Christobal
Villares de la Reina

Aldea Lengua

Aldea Rubia

Moriscos

Cabrerizos

Babila Fuente

R. Tormes

SALAMANCA

From Ciudad Rodrigo

St Marta

Calvarisa de abajo
Pelabravo

Huerba

Aldea Tejada

Las Torres

Machacon
Calvarrasa de arriba

PENARANDA de Bracamonte

Arapiles

R. Trabancos

ALBA DE TORMES

R. Tormes

R. Marganan

to Avila
to Madrid

MILES 5   0   5 MILES   London : Hugh Rees, Ltd.   Stanford's Geog¹ Estab¹ London.

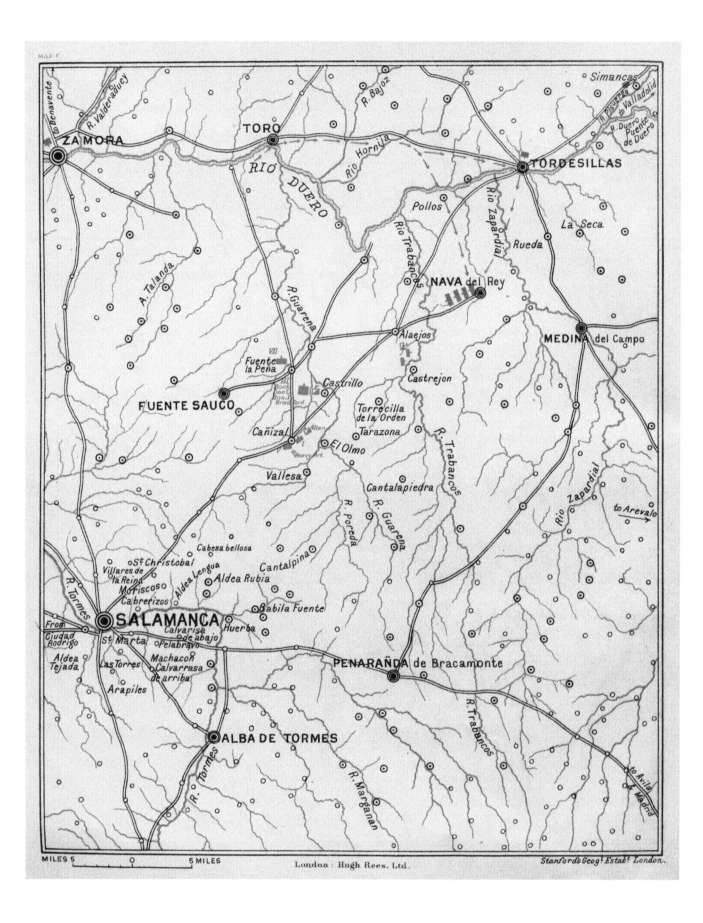

MAP F.

Simancas

R. Valderaduey
to Benavente
R. Pisuerga
to Valladolid
R. Duero de
Puente
de Duero

ZAMORA

TORO

TORDESILLAS

R. Bajoz

RIO

DUERO

Rio Hornija

Pollos

Rio Zapardial

La Seca

Rueda

A. Talanda

R. Guarena

Rio Trabancos

NAVA del Rey

FUENTE SAUCO

Fuente
la Peña

VII

Boch
Don C
Don J.
Bradford

Castrillo

Alaejos

Castrejon

MEDINA del Campo

Cañizal

Alten

El Olmo

Torrecilla
de la Orden

Tarazona

Vallesa

Cantalapiedra

R. Poreda

R. Guarena

R. Trabancos

Rio Zapardial

to Arevalo

Cabesa bellosa

St Christobal

Villares de
la Reina

Cantalpina

Aldea Lengua

Aldea Rubia

Moriscoso

Cabrerizos

R. Tormes

From
Ciudad
Rodrigo

SALAMANCA

St Marta

Babila Fuente

Calvarisa
de abajo
Pelabravo

Huerba

Aldea
Tejada

Las Torres

Machacon
Calvarrasa
de arriba

PENARANDA de Bracamonte

Arapiles

R. Trabancos

ALBA DE TORMES

R. Tormes

R. Marganan

to Avila
& Madrid

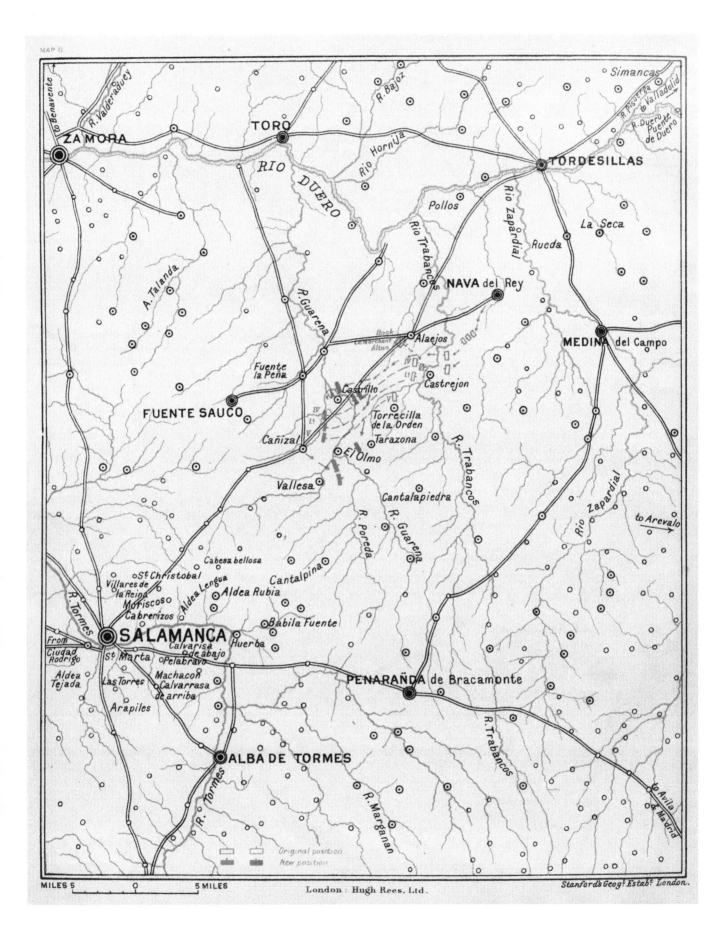

MAP 6

to Benavente
R. Valderaducy
ZAMORA
R. Tormes
From Ciudad Rodrigo
Aldea Tejada
St Marta
Las Torres
Arapiles
SALAMANCA
Calvarisa de abajo
Pelabravo
Machacon
Calvarrasa de arriba
Huerba
Villares de la Reina
St Christobal
Moriscos
Cabrerizos
Aldea Lengua
Aldea Rubia
Cantalpina
Babila Fuente
Cabesa bellosa
A. Talanda
R. Guarena
Fuente la Peña
FUENTE SAUCO
Cañizal
Vallesa
El Olmo
Castrillo
Torrecilla de la Orden
Tarazona
Cantalapiedra
R. Poreda
R. Guarena
R. Trabancos
Back to Merchant Alten
Alaejos
Castrejon
NAVA del Rey
Rio Trabancos
Pollos
TORO
RIO DUERO
Rio Hornija
Rio Hornija
R. Bajoz
Simancas
R. Pisverga to Valladolid
R. Duero Puente de Duero
TORDESILLAS
Rio Zapardial
Rueda
La Seca
MEDINA del Campo
Rio Zapardial
to Arevalo
ALBA DE TORMES
R. Tormes
PENARAÑDA de Bracamonte
R. Trabancos
R. Marganan
to Avila & Madrid

Original position
New position

MILES 5   0   5 MILES

London : Hugh Rees. Ltd.

Stanford's Geogl. Establt. London.

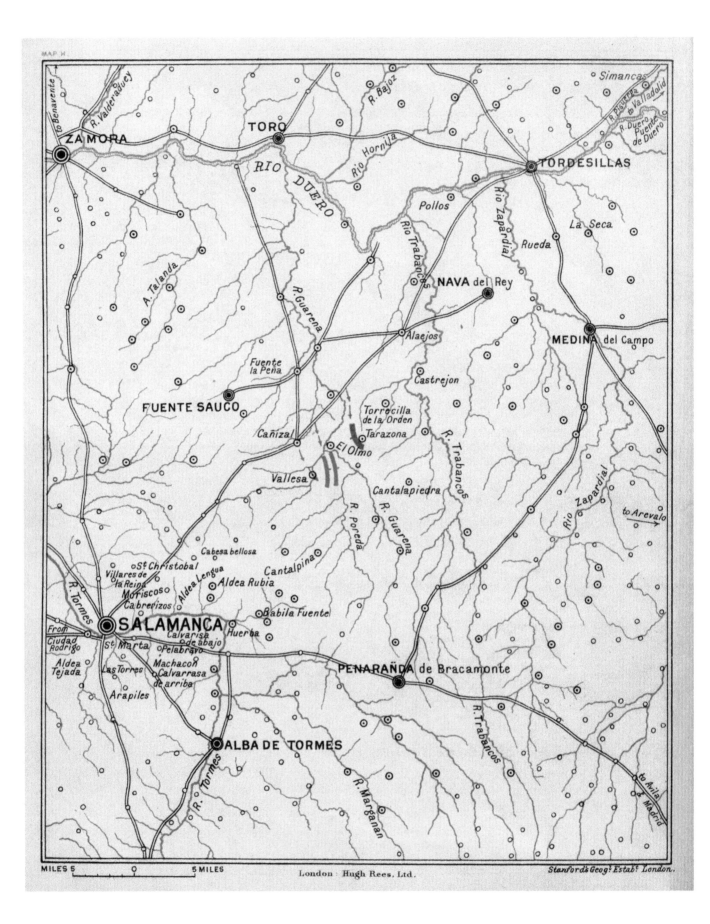

Simancas

R. Pisuerga
to Valladolid
R. Duero
Puente
de Duero

R. Valderaduey
to Benavente
ZAMORA
R. Valderaduey

TORO

TORDESILLAS

R. Bajoz

RIO

DUERO

Rio Hornija

Pollos

La Seca

Rio Zapardial

Rueda

Rio Trabancos

NAVA del Rey

MEDINA del Campo

R. Guarena

A. Talanda

Fuente
la Peña

Alaejos

Castrejon

FUENTE SAUCO

Torrecilla
de la Orden

Tarazona

R. Trabancos

Cañizal

El Olmo

Vallesa

Cantalapiedra

R. Poreda

R. Guarena

Rio Zapardial

to Arevalo

Cabesa bellosa

S.t Christobal

Villares de
la Reina

Moriscos

Aldea Lengua

Cantalpina

Aldea Rubia

R. Tormes

Cabrerizos

SALAMANCA

Babila Fuente

Huerba

From

Ciudad
Rodrigo

S.t Marta

Calvarisa
de abajo
Pelabravo

Aldea
Tejada

Las Torres

Machacon
Calvarrasa
de arriba

PENARANDA de Bracamonte

Arapiles

R. Trabancos

ALBA DE TORMES

R. Tormes

to Avila
& Madrid

R. Marganan

MILES 5   0   5 MILES

London : Hugh Rees, Ltd.

Stanford's Geog.l Estab.t London.

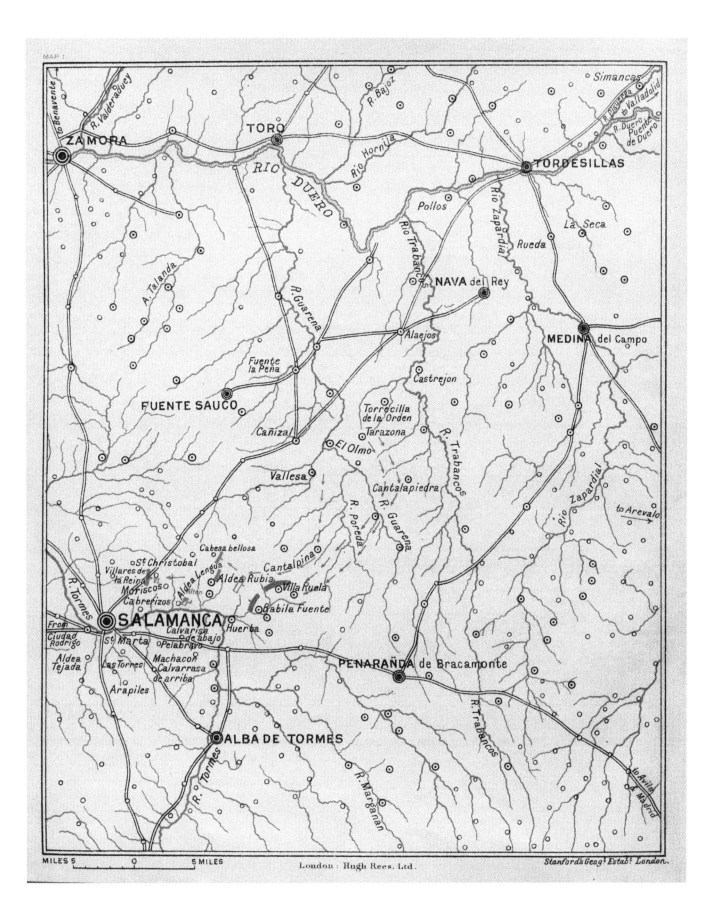

MAP 1.

to Benavente
R. Valderaduey
ZAMORA
R. Bajoz
Simancas
R. Piguerra
to Valladolid
R. Duero
Puente
de Duero
TORO
RIO
Rio Hornija
TORDESILLAS
DUERO
Pollos
Rio Zapardial
La Seca
Rueda
A. Talanda
R. Guarena
Rio Trabancos
NAVA del Rey
Alaejos
MEDINA del Campo
Fuente
la Pena
Castrejon
FUENTE SAUCO
Torrecilla
de la Orden
Tarazona
R. Trabancos
Cañizal
El Olmo
Cantalapiedra
Rio Zapardial
Vallesa
R. Poreda
R. Guarena
to Arevalo
Cabesa bellosa
oSt Christobal
Cantalpina
Villares de
la Reina
Aldea Lengua
Aldea Rubia
Moriscoso
Villa Ruela
Cabrerizos
Babila Fuente
R. Tormes
SALAMANCA
Huerba
From
Ciudad
Rodrigo
St Marta
Calvarisa
de abajo
oPelabravo
Aldea
Tejada
Las Torres
Machacon
Calvarrasa
de arriba
PENARAÑDA de Bracamonte
Arapiles
R. Trabancos
ALBA DE TORMES
R. Tormes
R. Marganan
to Avila
& Madrid

MILES 5   0   5 MILES   London : Hugh Rees. Ltd.   Stanford's Geog.l Estab.t London.

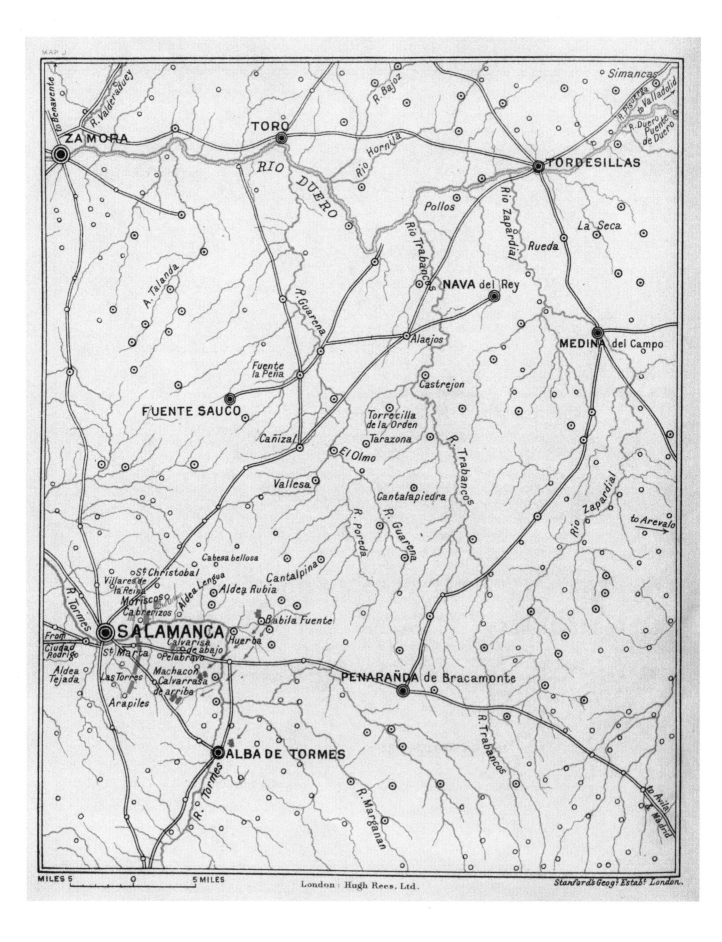

MAP J

to Benavente
R. Valderaduey
ZAMORA
R. Bajoz
Simancas
TORO
RIO
DUERO
Rio Hornija
TORDESILLAS
R. Pisuerga to Valladolid
R. Duero Puente de Duero
Pollos
Rio Zapardial
La Seca
Rueda
Rio Trabancos
R. Guarena
NAVA del Rey
Alaejos
MEDINA del Campo
Fuente la Peña
Castrejon
FUENTE SAUCO
Torrecilla de la Orden
Tarazona
R. Trabancos
Cañizal
El Olmo
Vallesa
Cantalapiedra
R. Poreda
R. Guarena
Rio Zapardial
to Arevalo
Cabesa bellosa
St Christobal
Villares de la Reina
Cantalpina
Aldea Lengua
Aldea Rubia
Moriscos
Cabrerizos
R. Tormes
SALAMANCA
Babila Fuente
From Ciudad Rodrigo
St Marta
Calvarisa de abajo
Huerba
Aldea Tejada
Pelabravo
Las Torres
Machacon
Calvarrasa de arriba
PEÑARAÑDA de Bracamonte
Arapiles
R. Trabancos
ALBA DE TORMES
R. Tormes
R. Marganan
to Avila & Madrid

MILES 5   0   5 MILES

London : Hugh Rees, Ltd.

Stanford's Geog¹ Estab¹ London.

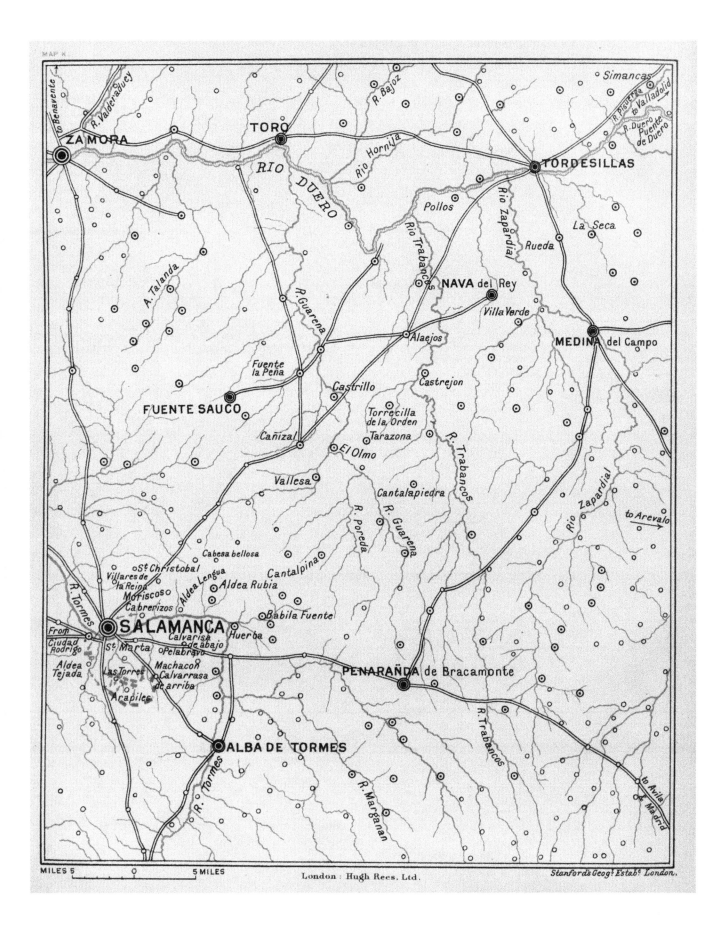

MAP K

ZAMORA

TORO

TORDESILLAS

Simancas

R. Pisuerga
to Valladolid

to Benavente

R. Valderaducy

R. Bajoz

RIO

DUERO

Rio Hornija

Pollos

Rio Zapardial

La Seca

Rueda

R. Duero
Puente
de Duero

Rio Trabancos

NAVA del Rey

A. Talanda

R. Guarena

Alaejos

Villa Verde

MEDINA del Campo

Fuente
la Peña

Castrillo

Castrejon

FUENTE SAUCO

Torrecilla
de la Orden

Cañizal

Tarazona

R. Trabancos

El Olmo

Vallesa

Cantalapiedra

R. Poreda

R. Guarena

Rio Zapardial

to Arevalo

Cabesa bellosa

Cantalpina

S? Christobal
Villares de
la Reina

Aldea Lengua

Aldea Rubia

Moriscoso
Cabrerizos

SALAMANCA

Babila Fuente

From
Ciudad
Rodrigo

S? Marta

Calvarisa
de abajo
o Pelabravo

Huerba

R. Tormes

Aldea
Tejada

Machacon
Calvarrasa
de arriba

Las Torres

PENARAÑDA de Bracamonte

Arapiles

R. Trabancos

ALBA DE TORMES

R. Tormes

R. Marganan

to Avila
& Madrid

MILES 5   0   5 MILES   London : Hugh Rees. Ltd.   *Stanfords Geog! Estab? London.*

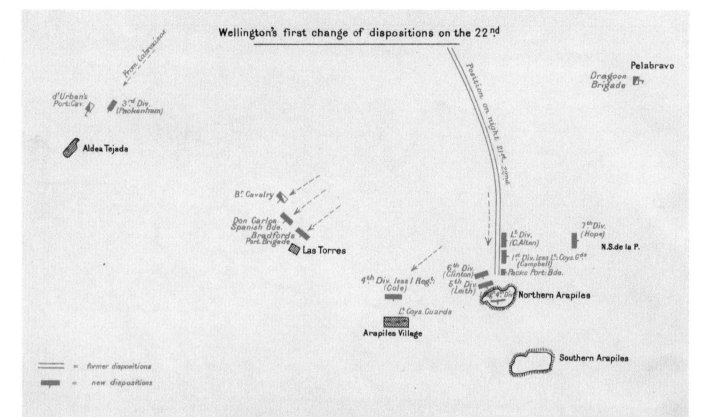

Wellington's first change of dispositions on the 22nd

From Calamoxicos

d'Urban's Port: Cav.   3rd Div. (Packenham)

Aldea Tejada

Bn Cavalry

Don Carlos Spanish Bde.
Bradfords Port. Brigade   Las Torres

4th Div. less 1 Regt. (Cole)
6th Div. (Clinton)
5th Div. (Leith)
3 & 4 Div   Northern Arapiles

Lt. Coys. Guards

Arapiles Village

Position on night 21st, 22nd

Lt. Div. (C. Alten)
7th Div. (Hope)
1st Div. less Lt. Coys. Gds (Campbell)   N.S.de la P.
Packs Port. Bde.

Pelabravo
Dragoon Brigade

Southern Arapiles

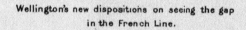

———— = former dispositions

▬▬ = new dispositions

Wellington's new dispositions on seeing the gap
in the French Line.

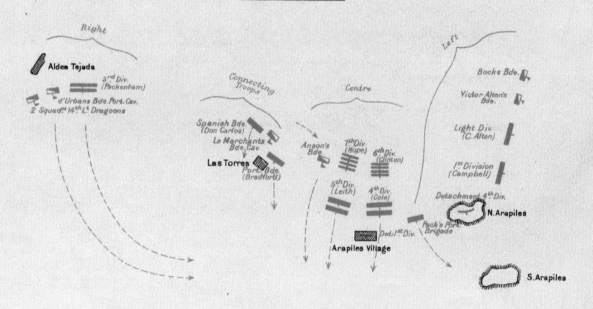

Right

Aldea Tejada

3rd Div. (Packenham)
d'Urbans Bde. Port. Cav.
2 Squadns 14th Lt. Dragoons

Connecting Troops

Centre

Left

Bocks Bde.

Victor Alten's Bde.

Spanish Bde. (Don Carlos)
Le Marchants Bde. Cav.
Las Torres
Port. Bde. (Bradford)

Anson's Bde.
7th Div. (Hope)
6th Div. (Clinton)

5th Div. (Leith)
4th Div. (Cole)

Detl. 1st Div.

Arapiles Village

Light Div. (C. Alten)

1st Division (Campbell)

Detachment 4th Div.   N. Arapiles

Pack's Port. Brigade

S. Arapiles

SKETCH MAPS (not drawn to scale) TO SHEW WELLINGTON'S DISPOSITIONS.

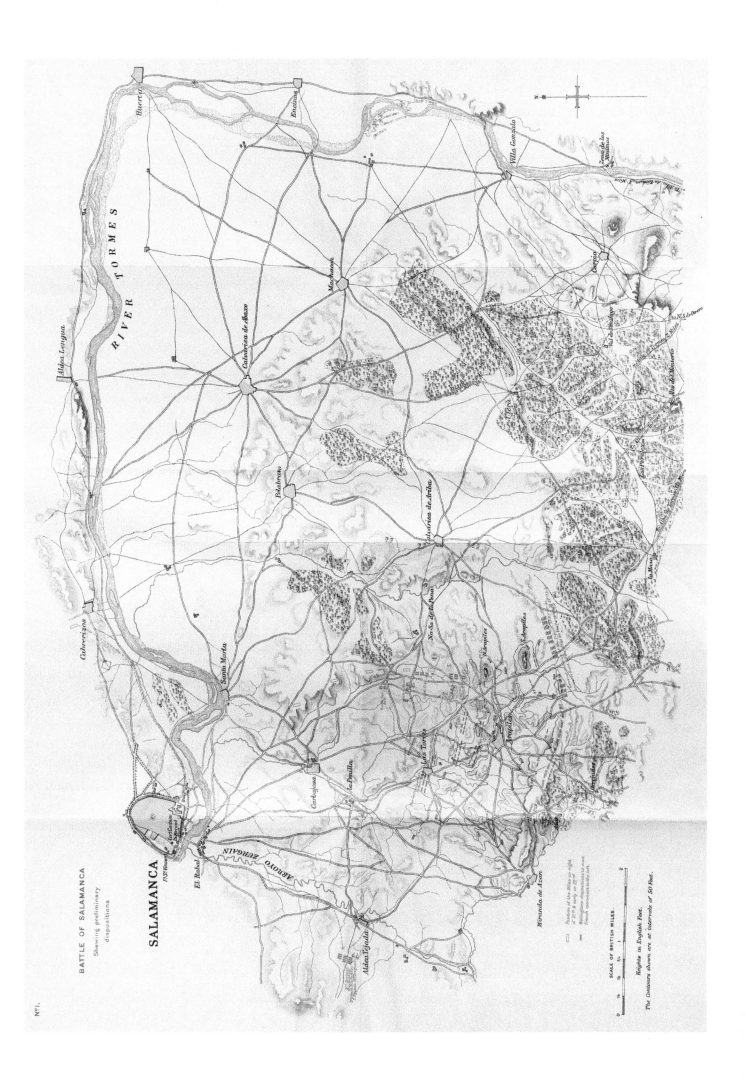

Nᵒ 1.

BATTLE OF SALAMANCA

Shewing preliminary
dispositions

SALAMANCA

RIVER TORMES

ARROYO ZURGAIN

SCALE OF BRITISH MILES.

0   ¼   ½   ¾   1   2

Heights in English Feet.

The Contours shown are at intervals of 50 Feet.

Position of the Allies on right
of 21ᵗ & early on 22ⁿᵈ

Mouvements afterwards in rear
French movements in red.

THE

SALAMANCA CAMPAIGN

NOTE.—In order not to confuse the historical account, comments and criticisms will be grouped together at the end of the two parts.

THE STRATEGY OF THE CAMPAIGN.

CHAPTER I.

GENERAL OUTLINE OF PRELIMINARY EVENTS.

IN order to obtain a clear idea of the Salamanca Campaign, **Introduction.** it is first necessary to have some knowledge of the events which preceded it. Only an outline of these will be given.

After the failure of Sir John Moore's campaign in 1808–9, **1808-9.** Sir A. Wellesley took command of the forces in Spain. He drove Soult out of Oporto, and marched on Madrid.

Soult, reinforced, concentrated, at Salamanca, on Wellesley's Line of Communications.

Wellesley, ignorant of this, drew up at Talavera to meet the attack of Victor (27th–28th July), won a great victory, but had to fall back to Portugal owing to Soult's presence on the flanks of his communications.

Napoleon was at this time able to throw a large army into Spain.

Wellington, recognising this, prepared the lines of Torres Vedras, and wintered at Almeida.

THE SALAMANCA CAMPAIGN.

Massena, with 70,000 men, advanced in the Spring of 1810. **1810.**

Wellington, giving up Ciudad Rodrigo, retired, devastating the country; he fought an action at Busaco, and then took refuge behind the lines of Torres Vedras.

Massena, failing to force these lines, and being barely able to keep his army from starvation, retreated as far as Santarem, where he maintained himself for the winter.

In the spring of 1811, Wellington was reinforced, and ad- **1811.** vanced. Massena retired, devastating the country. Though he had fought only one action, he had lost 30,000 men, chiefly from privation.

Soult, who was besieging Cadiz, was ordered to support Massena, but, after starting with part of his force and capturing Badajoz, he heard of Massena's retreat and returned to Cadiz.

Wellington spent the summer in attempting the capture of Almeida, Ciudad Rodrigo, and Badajoz, but only succeeded in the case of Almeida.

He defeated Massena at Fuentes d'Onoro, and Beresford defeated Soult at Albuera.

But Wellington was outnumbered, and retreated to cantonments on the Coa.

Wellington had from the first seen that, whatever number of **Strategical Note.** men Napoleon sent to Spain, they would have to separate to live, on account of the poverty of the country.

This was verified at the end of 1811. Soult moved South. Wellington thereupon resumed the offensive.

On January 19th Wellington took Ciudad Rodrigo by storm. **1812. Capture of Ciudad Rodrigo, Jan. 19th.** He thus opened the road to Spain, but it was also necessary to secure Portugal and the Lines of Communication by the capture of Badajoz.

Wellington completed the investment of Badajoz by the **Capture of Badajoz, April 6th, 1812.** middle of March, and, in order to capture it before Soult could arrive to relieve it, assaulted and carried it on the 6th of April, but the losses were terribly severe.

2

THE SALAMANCA CAMPAIGN.

The advance to Spain was now begun.

Massena fell under Napoleon's displeasure, and was succeeded by Marmont.

This brings us to the beginning of the Salamanca Campaign, **Notes.** and we may note the following points :—

(1.) Wellington's prevision in preparing the lines of Torres Vedras, and their effect.

(2.) The losses inflicted on the enemy by Wellington's waiting policy.

(3.) The importance to Wellington of a secure sea base.

(4.) The way in which Wellington's strategy depended on the knowledge that the enemy, having no proper base, must separate to live, and the way in which he waited, till they had so separated, to assume the offensive, thus bringing superior force to bear.

(5.) The importance, as pivots of manœuvre, of fortresses like Ciudad Rodrigo and Badajoz.

(6.) The fact that Wellington, who was usually careful of life, did not hesitate to risk fearful loss when an important object was in view, as at Badajoz.

CHAPTER II.

PRELIMINARY OPERATIONS — NUMBERS — CAPTURE OF ALMAREZ FORTS.

WELLINGTON's preparations for the siege of Badajoz had been made with the utmost secrecy, and every effort had been made to prevent the real object of the preparations being known.

On March 31st, Soult started to the relief of Badajoz, but on April 7th he heard it had fallen, and retired to Seville, which he reached on the 14th. Sir Stapleton Cotton, with 2000 cavalry, came up with him in his retreat near Usagre, and had a sharp and successful engagement with his rearguard. **1812.**
March 31st.

Usagre.

The effect of the capture of Ciudad Rodrigo and Badajoz in England and Spain was very great, and Napoleon could no longer ignore that affairs were going badly for him in the Peninsula. **April & May**

He argued that, if he, in person, descended on Spain, and Wellington retired again behind the impregnable lines of Torres Vedras, he would lose much prestige, which he could ill afford at this juncture. He determined, therefore, to cloak his inability to overwhelm the British and Portuguese armies by undertaking an action of superior éclat, viz., the invasion of Russia, leaving his Marshals to carry on the war in Spain. [See Jones.

Wellington was now tempted to attack Soult in Andalusia, but was prevented from doing so by news from the North. [Alison, Vol. IX., ch. xlviii., § 38.]

Marmont had advanced, by Napoleon's orders, from Salamanca, and entered Beira. Had he done this earlier in the year, he would probably have prevented the siege of Badajoz from taking place (*vide* Napier, Vol. IV., pp. 136, 137). Trant, Wilson, and Victor Alten had been forced to fall back before him across the Tagus, leaving the Northern provinces uncovered.

Moreover, the state of Ciudad Rodrigo and Almeida called for Wellington's attention. The Spaniards had not provisioned

4

the former, and the Portuguese had not put the latter in a state of defence as they had promised.

See Wellington's Despatches, Vol. IX. Letter to Lord Liverpool,*
      26th May, 1812.
        Alison, Vol. IX., chapter xlviii.
        Jones, chapter xiv.
        Maxwell, p. 273.
        Napier, Book XVI., chapter 7, also Book XVII., p. 152.

Wellington therefore decided to assume the offensive against **April 21st.** Marmont, in order to draw the enemy from the extremities of Spain.

After lingering a few days at Badajoz, he crossed the Tagus at Villa Velha, leaving Sir Thomas Graham with 10,000 men at Badajoz.

Marmont retired to Salamanca and the Douro, with his Divisions scattered but ready to concentrate (*vide* Marmont's Mémoires, Vol. IV., p. 207).

Both armies rested, Marmont on the Douro, and Wellington on the Mondego, Douro, and Tagus.

Wellington spent the interval in victualling and putting in a state of defence the various fortresses, arranging for supplies, and carrying out other preparations for his advance.

        *   *   *   *   *   *

We have now reached a convenient opportunity for considering **Numbers.** the composition of the opposing forces. This is a difficult matter, as the various authorities disagree, but we can hardly wonder at this when we remember that the French Army was an Army of Occupation, and when we consider how difficult it would be a hundred years hence to obtain an accurate idea of the numbers and situation of the various columns in South Africa at any particular time in 1900 or 1901.

---

* This letter is a fine example of an appreciation of the situation, and should be read carefully.

LAST RETURN OF THE BRITISH, HANOVERIAN, PORTUGUESE, AND SPANISH FORCES BEFORE
THE BATTLE OF SALAMANCA, DATED 11TH JULY, 1812.
FROM WELLINGTON'S SUPPLEMENTARY DESPATCHES, VOL. XIV., P. 61.

| | Officers. | N. C. O.'s. | Drummers and Trumpeters. | Rank and File. | | | | |
				Present.	Sick.	Command.	Prisoners of War.	Total.
Cavalry	211	248	46	3,986	596	924	27	5,533
*Artillery	181	76	33	2,610	478	1,338	...	4,426
Infantry	2,030	2,224	954	36,986	15,879	2,979	22	55,866
Spaniards { Cavalry	...	...	...	500	...	...	...	500
Spaniards { Infantry	...	...	...	3,000	...	...	...	3,000
Total	2,422	2,548	1,033	47,082†	16,953	5,241	49	69,325

* These returns include also the Artillery, Engineers, and Wagon trains in Estremadura under
Lt.-Gen. Sir Rowland Hill, K.B.
† This is shown in the despatches as 49,082.

EXTRACT FROM THE FRENCH IMPERIAL MUSTER ROLLS. GENERAL STATE OF THE
FRENCH ARMY, MAY 15TH, 1812.
FROM WELLINGTON'S SUPPLEMENTARY DESPATCHES, VOL. XIV. P. 59.

	Total Numbers.	Under Arms.
Army of the South	63,470	56,031
„ „ „ Centre	19,203	17,395
„ „ Portugal	70,700	52,618
„ „ Aragon...	35,377	27,218
„ „ Catalonia	41,530	36,677
„ „ the North	49,098	33,771
Total	279,378	225,710
Old Reserve of Bayonne...	6,500	3,894
New Reserve of Bayonne	5,769	2,598
Grand Total	291,647	232,202

THE SALAMANCA CAMPAIGN.

Alison's numbers are probably the most accurate, as they are based on all the available accounts, including the Imperial Muster Rolls, Jones, Napier, &c.

The 'state' given in Wellington's Supplementary Despatches, Vol. XIV., p. 61, does not quite agree, but it is interesting to note that the addition in this state is wrong by 2,000 men, the total rank and file 'present' being 47,082 instead of 49,082 as given. (*See opposite.*)

NUMBERS ACCORDING TO VARIOUS AUTHORITIES.

AUTHORITY.	ALLIES.	FRENCH.
ALISON.	53,000 British, of whom 7,500 Cavalry 27,000 Portuguese ——— 80,000 There were so many sick that the most Wellington could collect with the colours was 57,000, of whom 12,000 were with Hill and 45,000 with Wellington. Exact numbers of British were 53,169. *Vide* Adj.-Gen's. report.	About 40,000 were withdrawn in May, but the Imperial Muster Rolls still showed 280,000 soldiers in Spain, of whom 230,000 were present with the Colours. Details given later.
JONES.	'Wellington, after leaving 10,000 Infantry and 1,200 Cavalry to watch Soult, could muster 39,000 Infantry and 3,000 Cavalry.' 'The Spanish Army in Gallicia would occupy part of the enemy.'	'French forces exceeded 170,000 :— Soult ... ... 58,000 Marmont ... 55,000 Souhan ... ... 10,000 Suchet ... ... 40,000 Jourdan... ... 15,000 ———— 178,000
MORRIS. *Great Commanders.*	'About 40,000 with Wellington.'	'At least 250,000.'

6

THE SALAMANCA CAMPAIGN.

NUMBERS ACCORDING TO VARIOUS AUTHORITIES (*Continued*).

AUTHORITY.	ALLIES.	FRENCH.
MAXWELL.	Under Wellington's immediate command there were 75,328 (including 3,500 Spaniards) Of these 5,533 Cavalry 59 Guns. 16,958 rank and file were returned as sick on July 11th. Probably the effective was not more than 56,000. On the same date Hill's force was 25,146, including sick. Of these 2,576 Cavalry 14,192 { Portuguese Infantry 24 Guns. Also British garrison in Cadiz, Castaños' and Ballasteros' Spaniards, and the 7th Spanish Army; also Silveira's Portuguese Militia.	15th May. Soult ... ... 64,360 Marmont ... 69,037 Jourdan... ... 19,916 Souhan ... ... 53,276 Suchet ... ... 74,851 ———— 281,440 Spaniards ... 40,707 ———— 322,147 Also ... ... 12,000 on their way from France to reinforce Marmont.
GLEIG.	Actually present with Wellington ... ... 56,000 Not including 6,000 in Cadiz but including 24,000 Portuguese Hill's Corps— 18,000 Infantry 2,000 Cavalry 24 Guns. Total strength at Headquarters was 36,000 Infantry, 3,500 Cavalry, 54 Guns. Add 3,500 Spaniards under d'España and Sanchez, making 42,500, not 55,000 as Thiers says. Fully one-third English were in hospital.	Marmont ... ... 52,000 Soult ... ... 56,000 Suchet ... ... 60,000 Caffarelli ... ... 38,000 Jourdan ... ... 17,000 ———— 215,000

THE SALAMANCA CAMPAIGN.

NUMBERS ACCORDING TO VARIOUS AUTHORITIES (*Continued*).

AUTHORITY.	ALLIES.	FRENCH.
NAPIER. Vol. IV., p. 219 p. 226	90,000 Anglo-Portuguese, including 6,000 at Cadiz, but there were only effective 32,000 British and 24,000 Portuguese, making a total of 56,000.	In May there were nearly 300,000 French troops and 40,000 Spaniards.

Under Napier (Allies):

	UNDER HILL.	UNDER WELLINGTON.
	2,000 Cav.	3,500 Cav. ⎫
	15,000 Inf.	36,000 Inf. ⎬ Br.
	24 Guns	54 Guns ⎭
	also Spaniards	3,500 Spaniards
	17,000 + Guns	43,000 + Guns

Also 12,000 Portuguese Cavalry in the Tras Os Montes.

Under Napier (French):

	Total.	Effective.
Suchet...	76,000	60,000
Caffarelli	49,000	38,000
Jourdan	19,000	17,000
Soult ...	63,000	56,000
Marmont	70,000	52,000
+	12,000	12,000
	289,000	235,000

AUTHORITY.	ALLIES.	FRENCH.
THIERS.	British Infantry, 7 Divisions, 35,000 to 36,000. Cavalry 5,000 to 6,000. Plus Portuguese and Spaniards. Total about 55,000. *See* Vol. XLVI., p. 76.	300,000, of whom 230,000 effective. *See* Vol. XLVI., pp. 40–58, for details as to distribution and duties of the Armies, and the difficulties of Command. *See* also extract in footnote on p. 11.

The French forces were divided into five Armies, which were **Dispositions and Plans.** situated as follows :—

DESIGNATION.	COMMANDER.	WHERE SITUATED.
Army of Catalonia ...	Suchet ...	Catalonia and Valencia
Army of the North ...	Caffarelli ...	Biscay and Navarre, 2 Divisions detached to reinforce Marmont
Army of the Centre ...	Jourdan ...	Madrid
Army of the South ...	Soult ...	Andalusia and Estremadura
Army of Portugal ...	Marmont ...	Leon, Old Castille, Asturias

These Armies will be dealt with in detail later. *Vide* p. 11.

THE SALAMANCA CAMPAIGN.

It will be seen that the French were widely scattered, while Wellington was in a central position, with sea base and water carriage in his rear.

The question for Wellington to decide now was whether to deliver a blow against Marmont in the North or Jourdan in the Centre. Wellington, as indeed did Napoleon, looked on the line of communications from Bayonne to Madrid as vital to the French Armies, and therefore decided that a greater result would be obtained by attacking Marmont. *[See Despatches, Vol. IX., May 26th, 1812, June 14th, June 18th.]*

It had been arranged that 10,000 British troops from Sicily and 6,000 Spaniards from Majorca should be disembarked on the East coast of Spain, and should raise Catalonia and Valencia in arms, uniting with the remnants of Blake's army under O'Donnell. **Proposed diversion on the East Coast.**

The effect of this would be (1) to contain Suchet on the East, (2) to prevent the Army of the Centre under Jourdan from leaving the neighbourhood of Madrid, whence it could reinforce the East if necessary.

In the meantime, Wellington sent Hill to attack the French bridge-heads and forts at Almarez on the Tagus, which covered the only crossing by which Soult and Marmont could communicate by a short line. **The Almarez Operations.**

This was a difficult operation, because:—

(1) Drouet, with 9,000 of Soult's army, was at Hinojoza.

(2) Foy's division of Marmont's army was in the valley of the Tagus.

(3) D'Armagnac was at Talavera.

However, Hill, marching from Almandraleja, via Jaraicejo, stormed the bridge-head forts (Fort Napoleon and Fort Ragusa), on May 19th, and captured all the artillery and an immense quantity of stores. **Hill's capture of the Almarez Forts, May 19th.**

He also nearly captured Fort Mirabete, but was obliged to leave it owing to a false report of the approach of Soult.

He retired to Merida, which he reached safely on May 26th.

THE SALAMANCA CAMPAIGN.

For details of this very fine operation read Napier, Vol. IV., pp. 159–167; and Alison, Vol. IX., ch. lxviii., § 46–50.

Having thus destroyed the shortest line of communication between two portions of the enemy's forces, Wellington caused the bridge at Alcantara to be repaired, in order to improve and shorten the communications between his own forces. **Repair of the Alcantara Bridge.**

For details see Napier, Vol. IV., p. 224.

Meantime, a rash attack by Spaniards under Ballasteros on a French detachment at Bornos, between Cadiz and Seville, had been severely defeated. **Unfortunate Spanish action in the South.**

This relieved Soult's anxiety about his rear, and he was able to reinforce Drouet in Estremadura.

Matters now looked serious for the Allies in Estremadura. Wellington increased Hill's force to :— **Situation in Estremadura.**

20,000 British and Portuguese ⎫
3,000 Spaniards ⎭ of whom 2,500 were cavalry.

Thus Hill and Drouet contained one another near Albuera.

Hill's self-effacement at this time, in merely keeping his wicket up and not attempting to score himself, is worthy of note, and in contrast to the jealousies of the French Marshals, especially at a time when his brilliant exploit at Almarez had brought his name prominently to the front. **Note.**

Read Napier, Vol. IV., p. 194; and Alison, Vol. IX., ch. xlviii., § 52.

THIERS, IN VOL. XLVI., PAGE 40, *et seq.*, GIVES THE FOLLOWING DISTRIBUTION,
WHICH IS INTERESTING, AS IT SUPPLIES SOME DETAILS.

NAME.	GENERAL.	LOCALITY.	TOTAL.	REMARKS.
Army of North ...	Dorsenne ... (Succeeded by Cafarelli. *Vide* Marmont's Life, Book XV.)	Navarre, Biscay, and Old Castille, Including the garrisons of Bayonne... ... ... St. Sebastian ... ... Pampeluna ... ... Bilbao ... ... Tolosa ... ... Vittoria ... ... Burgos ... ... Leaving for Field Army only 25,000	—46,000	Operating against the guerilla chiefs, Mina, &c.
Army of Portugal	Marmont ...	With Bonnet in Asturias 7,000 In Astorga ... ... 1,500 Zamora ... ... 500 Leon .. .. 500 Valladolid ... ... 1,000 Salamanca ... ... 1,000 Small posts ... ... 1,500 L. of C. ... ... 2,000 Field Army 37,000	—52,000	
Army of Centre ...	Joseph	His own army .. ... 14,000 From Soult's army .. 2,000 Spaniards. paid by Joseph 3,000	—19,000	
Army of Andalusia	Soult	Cadiz (for siege) ... 12,000 Grenada (for defence) 10,000 Arcos (for patrolling) ... 5,000 Estremadura (under d'Erlon, for containing Hill) ... ... 15,000 Cavalry ... ... 2,000 to 3,000 Field Army near Seville 14,000	—58,000	
Army of Arragon	Suchet	In Aragon, under Reille 14,000 In Catalonia, under Decaen ... ... 27,000 On L. of C. along Mediterranean, especially near Alicante, 16,000 to 17,000 Field Army ... 7,000 to 8,000	—64,000	
			239,000	

CHAPTER III.

SOULT had for a long time been maturing a plan for invading *Soult's* Portugal from the South. His plan, briefly, was as follows ;— *plan.*

[Napier, Vol. IV., pp. 189, 190.

   (1) To crush Ballasteros.
   (2) To reduce Tarifa, Alicante, and Carthagena.
   (3) Then to leave Andalusia to be defended by Victor
        with 20,000 Spanish troops, locally raised,
   (4) and attack Portugal with 40,000 men.

Wellington had, however, been pushing on his preparations, *Initiative.* and, though Soult's first object had been nearly gained by the rash action of Ballasteros at Bornos, yet Wellington was able to gain the initiative.

At this time the situation and numbers were approximately *Recapitula-* as follows :— *tion of numbers and disposition.*

FRENCH.

GENERALS.	TOTAL NOS.	EFFECTIVE.	LOCALITY.
Suchet ...	76,000 ...	60,000 ...	Catalonia and Valencia.
Caffarelli ...	49,000 ...	33,000* ...	Biscay and Navarre.
Jourdan ...	19,000 ...	17,000* ...	Madrid.
Soult ...	63,000 ...	56,000 ...	Andalusia and S. Estremadura.
Marmont ...	70,000 ...	52,000 ...	Leon and Old Castille.
	277,000	218,000	
	12,000	12,000	marching to reinforce Marmont.
Total ...	289,000	230,000	

To this add 40,000 Spaniards for what they were worth.

ALLIES.

Effective, about 40,000 with Wellington.
20,000 with Hill.

* According to Alison, Caffarelli had 38,000, and Jourdan, 19,000. The numbers given above, however, are taken from the General State.

For details of the distribution, *see table opposite.*

11

THE SALAMANCA CAMPAIGN.

Though there was such a disparity in the numbers, the British **Moral and other factors affecting the situation.** force had the advantage of being confident (*vide* Despatches), skilfully led, amply supplied, possessing internal L. of C., enjoying the confidence of the inhabitants. Moreover, it was commanded by one man, who was ably seconded by his subordinates.

The French Commanders, on the other hand, were jealous of one another, and paid little attention to Joseph and Jourdan.

[*Vide* Marmont's Correspondence.]

Marmont's divisions at this time were scattered, but within concentrating distance of one another. They were situate as follows :— **8th June. Position of Marmont's Divisions.**

1st Division	...	...	...	Avilo Arivalo
2nd „	...	...	...	Penaranda and Fontiveros
3rd „	...	...	...	Valladolid
4th „	...	...	...	Toro
5th „	...	...	...	} Salamanca
6th „	...	...	...	
7th „	...	...	...	Zamora
8th „	...	...	...	in Asturias
Light Cavalry	...	...	Salamanca
Dragoons	...	...	...	Toro and Benavente
Headquarters ...	...	...	Salamanca

On June 13th Wellington crossed the Agueda and com-**June 13th to 17th. Wellington's advance.** menced his offensive movement, reaching Salamanca on June 17th.

He crossed the river Tormes in four columns at the fords of St. Marta and Los Cantos. [*See* Sup. Despatches, Vol. XIV., No. 1179, 1182. Despatches (Garwod), Vol. IX., June 18th, to Lord Liverpool.

On June 14th Marmont retired to Bleines, throwing garrisons into the forts at Salamanca and Alba de Tormes, and ordering a general concentration of his Divisions. The 8th Division was **June 14th. Marmont retires.** specially ordered to join by forced marches from Asturias.

The Allied Army 'took position on the heights of St. **June 19th. Covering position.** Christoval, three miles in advance of the town, with its right on the Tormes near Cabrezizos, and left near Villares de la Regna.' [Jones.]

THE SALAMANCA CAMPAIGN.

The French had built and garrisoned three strong forts, named **Siege of the forts.** St. Vincent, Cajetano, and La Meread. These were immediately invested by the Allied Forces, but they proved unexpectedly strong, and the British were short of breaching guns.

Marmont, having taken steps to collect on the Douro between **Marmont's advance to the relief of the forts.** [Alison, Vol. IX., ch. lxviii., § 35.] the 16th and 19th the whole of his Army, except Bonnet's Division, which was still in Asturias, advanced to the relief of the forts. His force, so far concentrated, consisted of the 2nd, 3rd, 4th, 5th, 6th Infantry Divisions, and one Cavalry Brigade, in all about 25,000 men.

Wellington had ordered the guerillas to harass his rear, but this had had but little effect.

Marmont drove in the British advanced post, and occupied the **June 20th.** village of Moresco, in front of the Allied position.

Wellington expected attack, and concentrated on St. Chris- [Despatches, Vol. IX., June 25th, 1812, to Earl of Liverpool.] toval, passing the night in bivouac. (For a very good description of this position see Napier, Vol. IV., p. 238.)

Marmont, however, did not attack, but in the evening of the **June 21st.** 21st there was a partial engagement, made to dislodge Marmont from the village of Moresco.

The criticisms passed on Wellington for not attacking Marmont on this date will be considered later (p. 42).

On June 22nd Marmont was reinforced:— **June 22nd.**

> According to Alison: by two Divisions of Infantry and one Brigade of Cavalry, bringing his force up to 'nearly 40,000 men, of whom 3,200 Cavalry and 72 guns.'
>
> According to Gleig: 'Reinforcements to about 36,000 men.'
>
> According to Napier: '3 Divisions Infantry and 1 Brigade Cavalry . . . nearly 40,000.'
>
> According to Marmont: No reinforcements mentioned.

On this day there was some manœuvring and skirmishing, but Marmont, finding the British position too strong to be attacked, fell back during the night of the 22nd–23rd, and in the evening of the 23rd occupied a position about Aldea Rubia, with the right flank at Cabeza Vellosa and the left at Huerta. **June 23rd.** [Despatches, Vol. IX., June 25th, to Earl of Liverpool. Also Napier, Vol. IV., p. 240.]

Wellington sent Bock's German Horse across the Tormes to observe the passages of the river, and changed front with his right at St. Marta, and advanced troops at Aldea Lengua, so that he could manœuvre on either bank of the Tormes.

On this day an unsuccessful assault was made on the forts, led by General Bowes, who was killed.

About 2 a.m. on the 24th Marmont sent 12,000 men across the river, and prepared to follow with the rest of the Army, pushing back Bock's Cavalry, who retired in good order. **June 24th.**

Wellington sent two Divisions Infantry and a Cavalry Brigade (1st and 7th Divisions and Le Marchant's Cavalry Brigade) under Sir Thomas Graham, across the river at St. Marta, while the remainder of the Allies concentrated between Moresco and Cabrezizos. The advanced troops remained at Aldea Lengua.

The French troops pushed on as far as Calvarisa de Abaxo, but, finding the force under Sir T. Graham in order of battle, and the other British Divisions ready to cross, they halted, and in the evening recrossed at Huerta and occupied their former position about Aldea Rubia, or, as Napier describes it, in front of Velares.

Criticisms have also been directed against Wellington for not attacking Marmont on this date. These will be considered later.

There was a delay in the prosecution of the siege of the forts owing to want of ammunition; but on the 26th this arrived from Almeida. **June 26th.**

On the night of June 26th, and morning of June 27th, St. Vincent Fort was set on fire by red-hot shells, and on the 27th the three forts were taken by assault. 700 prisoners, 30 guns, and a large quantity of stores were captured. **June 27th. Capture of the forts.**

The Allies had lost in the siege, and in covering it, about 500 men. [Despatches, Vol. IX. Letter of 30th June, to Earl of Liverpool.]

Marmont explains in his letter of June 30th to the Minister of War, that he would have fought on the 23rd if he had not heard that Caffarelli was on his way to join him. This caused him to retire to Villa (Aldea) Rubia, to avoid premature action. On the 26th, Marmont no longer expected Cafarelli, and, hearing by signal from the forts that they could hold out for three days, determined to attack on the 28th, but was anticipated by the unexpected fall of the forts on the 27th.

[Sup. Despatches, Vol. XIV. Marmont's Letter, June 8th. Napier, Vol. IV., pp 243-4.

On hearing of the capture of the forts, Marmont retired behind the Douro, withdrawing the garrison from Alba de Tormes. His marches were as follows :—

Marmont's retreat, June 28th to July 2nd. [Marmont's Memoirs]

> June 28th.   To the Guarema.
> „   29th.   To the Trabancos.
> „   30th.   No move.
> July 1st.   To the Zapardiel.

He was followed by the Allies, who marched as follows :—

> June 30th.   To the Guarema, in three columns.
> July 1st.   To the Trabancos, in three columns—Advanced guard at Nava del Rey.

[For details, see Sup. Despatches, Vol. XIV. No. 1184, 1185.]

> „   2nd.   Passed the Zapardiel in two columns, the right by Medina de Campo and the left towards Rueda. On this day the advanced guard, under Sir Stapleton Cotton, drove the French rearguard across the river at Tordesillas.

[Despatches, Vol. IX., July 7th, to Earl Bathurst.]

In the meantime the Army of Gallicia, under General Santocildes, had been blockading Astorga, and now that the fall of the Salamanca forts made his operations secure, commenced serious preparations for its reduction.

Astorga besieged. [Despatches, Vol. IX., 7th and 14th July, to Earl Bathurst.]

Other Spanish and Portuguese forces were at Cervajales, Castromonte, and Palencia.

Marmont concentrated between Pollos and Tordesillas, with his left at Simancas on the Pisuerga, with the bridges at Simancas and Puente de Duero guarded by fortified posts, and with strong posts at Zamora and Toro. Here he awaited reinforcements from :—

Marmont's dispositions

(1) Bonnet, from the Asturias. (On his way.)

THE SALAMANCA CAMPAIGN.

(2) Caffarelli, from Biscay.   (Supposed to be marching to join him.)

[Marmont's Memoirs, pp. 221 to 224.]

(3) Joseph, from Madrid.   (Should have been in motion by now.)

Wellington took up his position on the left bank of the Douro, from La Seca to Pollos, whilst preparing to force a passage, and waited for the river to go down.

Wellington's dispositions [Despatches, Vol. IX., July 7th. 8th. and 9th.]

Headquarters at Rueda.

The head   at the ford of Pollos and the bridge of Tordesillas.

The rear   at Medina del Campo, and other points on the Zapardiel and Trabancos rivers, to watch any movement from the Valladolid side.

There were few bridges or fords, and the French position, which was very strong, was guarded by 100 guns.

Wellington hoped that, from want of supplies, Marmont would have to fall back or separate.

He let loose the Guerillas on Marmont's flanks and rear—to make him separate his forces or make a decisive movement, to cut his supplies and render large detachments necessary for their collection.

On July 7th, Marmont was joined by Bonnet's Division, making his strength, according to Alison, 44,000 men, and according to Jones, 47,000. Napier, on p. 247, Vol. IV., traces the failure of Caffarelli to reinforce Marmont later on to the fact of Bonnet's Division having been withdrawn from Asturias.

July 7th to 15th.

At this time, however, Caffarelli, with 10,000 infantry and 1,500 cavalry, was reported to be approaching.

Wellington's supplies were being brought up by a long line of communications, which would be threatened if the Army of the Centre advanced from Madrid.

16

CHAPTER IV.

MARMONT'S ADVANCE ACROSS THE DOURO—DAILY MOVEMENTS
BETWEEN JULY 15TH AND JULY 22ND.

WE now come to the events more immediately leading up to
the battle. These can best be shown by a series of maps copied
from the Geological Survey of Spain. This is the only map that
can be regarded as giving the position of the towns and villages
accurately, as the Ordnance Survey of Spain has never been completed. Unfortunately it does not give the hill features, and these
can only be inferred from the watercourses.

It is owing to this lack of good maps that the campaign and
some of the criticisms passed on it are so difficult to understand.
For instance Napier, in Vol. IV., p. 258, says that on the 16th July
Marmont, having crossed the Douro, was actually nearer Salamanca than the Allies were; but this statement is not borne out
when the distances are measured on the Geological Survey map.
In Napier's map, facing page 253, Castrejon is shown as being
further from Salamanca than Toro, whereas the contrary is the
case.

In the following maps only those places are named which are
referred to in the text, but the same conventional sign is used for
villages and towns as in the original, so that the student, if he
wishes to add names referred to in other books, may readily
identify them on reference to the Geological Survey map.

THE SALAMANCA CAMPAIGN.

15TH JULY.

The French positions are described on p. 15. It only remains to add that the Pisuerga was unfordable, and that the bridges even at Valladolid and Simancas were held as fortified posts.

The bridges over the Douro at Zamora, Toro, Puente de Duero, and Tudela had been broken.

The bridge at Tordesillas had been preserved.

There was a ford at Pollos. This had been seized by the 3rd Division under Packenham.

On the 8th, after the arrival of Bonnet's Division, Marmont had extended to the right, and commenced repairing the bridge at Toro.

Writing on July 21st, Wellington says : ' It was totally out of my power to prevent the enemy from passing the Douro at any point at which he might think it expedient, as he had in his possession all the bridges over that river and many of the fords.' [Despatches, July 21st, to Earl Bathurst.]

Realising this, on July 12th Wellington issued a memorandum giving instructions for the movements of his troops under various eventualities. This memorandum should be carefully studied, as it bore fruit on the 16th. It should be noted that this memorandum was addressed to the Q.M.Gen., and that he issued the orders. [Supplementary Despatches, Vol. XIV., No 1190.]

THE SALAMANCA CAMPAIGN.

16TH JULY.

During the 15th and 16th Marmont concentrated between Toro and the Hornija River, and on the 16th it was reported to Wellington:—

(1) That at Tordesillas only the garrison was left.

(2) That two Divisions had crossed at Toro.

Wellington moved to Fuente la Pena and Canizal on the night of the 16th, uniting his centre and left at these places, but, as he had some doubts as to the enemy's real object, he left:—

4th Division (Lt.-Gen. Cole)
Light Division (Lt.-Gen. C. Alten) } under Sir Stapleton Cotton,
Anson's Cavalry

at Castrejon, on the Trabancos, 12 miles N.E.

The hasty orders issued for these movements on the night of the 16th are given in Wellington's Supplementary Despatches, Vol. XIV., No. 1192, as follows:—

1st Division to Alacjos.

7th   „   to Fuente la Pena as soon as 1st Div. crosses the Trabancos.

3rd   „
Bock's Brigade
Don Carlos d'Espagna's Inf. } to Castrillo on the Guarema.
Don Gulian's Cav.
Bradford's Bde.

4th Division
Light Division } to Castrejon.

5th Division to Canizal, leaving Alacjos on the right, as soon as 4th and Light Divs. have quitted Villa Verde.

1st Division from Alacjos to Canizal as soon as troops under Lt.-Gen. Picton and the 5th Div. have passed Alacjos.

Alten's Cavalry to Alecjos, and afterwards to follow 1st Div.

Anson's Cavalry from Medina to Castrejon.

Then follow details as to baggage, etc.

19

THE SALAMANCA CAMPAIGN.

17TH JULY.

The French recrossed the river during the night of the 16th–17th at Toro, destroying the bridge, and marched by forced marches to Tordesillas, 25 miles above Toro.

The whole French army crossed here and at Pollos without opposition, and reached Nava del Rey that night, and the Trabancas early on the 18th. Total distance 40 miles.

Wellington was then near Toro, and news of this movement did not reach him till near midnight on the 17th.

The troops under Lt.-Gen. Sir Stapleton Cotton remained at Castrejon without orders and in a bad position on the night of the 17th.

This manœuvre· of Marmont reduced Wellington to great **Note.** difficulties. It established communication between Marmont and Joseph, who was behind the Guadarama Pass. If this junction were effected, and Caffarelli also arrived, it would raise the French [Alison.] force to 70,000 men and 140 guns.

Moreover, at this time, bad news reached Wellington from all sides :—

The Spaniards would not assault Astorga.

The guerilla Mina had been badly defeated in the North.

The news from Cadiz was bad.

Lord William Bentinck, instead of making a diversion on the [Despatches. Vol. IX., July 14th, to Earl Bathurst.]
    East coast of Spain, sailed for Italy.

Remittances of money had not come from home; his troops
    and muleteers were in arrears of pay.

THE SALAMANCA CAMPAIGN.

18TH JULY.

Wellington hastened in person to the right, ordering Bock's, Le Marchant's, and Alten's Cavalry Brigades to follow him to Alacjos, and the 5th Division to take post at Torrecilla de la Orden.

[Despatches, July 21st, Earl Bathurst: Napier, Vol. IV.; Alison, Vol IX., ch. lxviii., § 64.]

Cotton maintained his position from daylight till 7 a.m. (for description of the fight see Napier, Vol. IV., pp. 256–258).

Wellington arrived on the scene, and about this time Marmont, seeing that he had only part of the British Army before him, crossed the Trabancos in two columns, turned the British left, and marched towards the Guarema. The British retired, picking up the 5th Division on the way, and covered by the Cavalry.

The two forces raced parallel to one another, apparently fighting most of the time. So closely were the British pressed that they were fired on by 40 guns as they crossed the Guarema between Olmo and Castrillo. But they succeeded in joining the rest of the Army on the heights on the left bank.

On Marmont's main force coming up, he attempted to gain the Vallesa heights. He sent Clausel to make a feint on the right against the ridge above Castrillo between the Guarema and the stream from Canizal.

Wellington had meantime sent the other Divisions from Canizal to occupy the Vallesa heights.

Just as the 4th Division gained the heights of Canizal, Clausel sent Carrier's Brigade of Cavalry across at Castrillo, and supported it with a column of Infantry.

Alten's Dragoons charged them, but the enemy were reinforced. Wellington then sent the 27th and 40th Regiments and the 3rd Dragoons to support the cavalry, and the enemy were driven back.

Marmont withdrew the troops he had sent towards Vallesa,

and concentrated at Castrillo in such a way as to hold both banks.

The French lost 1 G.O.C., 300 men killed, 1 gun, and 240 prisoners.

The Allies lost during the day 100 killed, 400 wounded, 50 prisoners.

---

(1) Note the dispositions of Wellington to cover the retreat of **Notes.** the right wing, shown clearly on the sketch map.

(2) Note the steadiness of the retirement and the discipline which must have existed.

(3) Note the recognition of both Commanders of the important point to seize, and how Wellington, divining that Marmont would try and seize the Vallesa heights, forestalled him by sending there the troops that had been at Canizal all day.

(4) Note that Wellington, though his right had been turned and he was facing to a flank, still covered his communications.

THE SALAMANCA CAMPAIGN.

19TH JULY.

Both Armies remained quiet till the afternoon. About 4 o'clock Marmont moved to his left on Tarazona, with a view to crossing the river higher up.

Wellington, fearing for his right, crossed the branch of the Guarema at Vallesa and El Olmo, and took post on the high ground above those villages. The Guarema here consists of two branches, the upper and the lower, enclosing the Vallesa tableland. There was an interchange of artillery fire, and preparations were made for battle.

The Allies were formed in two lines, and Wellington expected to be attacked, as the range of heights which he occupied trended back to the Tormes, and he thought Marmont could not turn his right on account of the Spanish garrison which he had thrown into Alba de Tormes.

This garrison, however, had been withdrawn by Carlos d'Espagna. The time at which this occurred, whether Marmont knew of it, and why Wellington did not know about it, will be discussed later.

THE SALAMANCA CAMPAIGN.

20TH JULY.

At daybreak, instead of crossing the Guarema and attacking, Marmont marched in several columns, covered by a powerful rearguard, to Catalpiedra, where he crossed, and gained another range of hills leading to the Tormes, parallel to those from Vallesa.

The Allies made a corresponding movement to their right, marching in two lines, and tried to cross the march of the French at Catalpino; but at this point it was evident that they had been outmarched and outflanked. Wellington fell off to his right, towards the heights of Cabeça Vellosa and Aldea Rubia, where he intended to halt, while the 6th Division and Alten's Cavalry seized Aldea Lengua and the position of St. Christoval. But he did not seize the ford at Huerta, as he did not think the French could reach it.

In the evening his second line had reached the Cabeça Vellosa heights, but his first line was in the low ground towards Hornillos. It then appeared from the French bivouac fires that the enemy were extended in a half-circle from Villa Ruela to Babila Fuente, and commanded the ford of Huerta.

Wellington then, under cover of the smoke of his bivouac fires, moved hastily towards Cabeça Vellosa and Aldea Rubia.

Marmont had outmarched and outflanked the Allies, and had **Notes.** gained command of the Tormes. His junction with the Army of the Centre was secured, and he could fight, continue manœuvring, or await reinforcements, as he pleased.

Wellington was now almost facing the opposite way to that in which he had been facing on the Douro; he was, at all events, facing in a direction parallel with his communications.

He prepared to retire to Portugal, but fully realised what the [Despatches, Vol. IX. *Vide* concluding paragraphs of letter of 21st July.] moral and political effect of this would be.

THE SALAMANCA CAMPAIGN.

21st JULY.

The Allies took up their old position of St. Christoval.

The French threw a garrison into Alba de Tormes, and then crossed the Tormes between Alba and Huerta, moved up the valley of the Machacon, and encamped with their leading Divisions behind Calvarisa de Ariba. One Division was left on the heights of Babila Fuente.

In the evening, Wellington made a corresponding flank march by the bridges and fords of St. Marta and Aldea Lengua, and took up, approximately, the same position as Graham had occupied the previous month.

The left rested on the Tormes, near St. Marta, with a cavalry post advanced towards Calvarisa de Abaxo and Pelabravo. The right extended along some heights, which ended half a mile from the village of Arapiles.

This position covered Salamanca.

The 3rd Division (Packenham's), and D'Urban's Cavalry, remained on the right bank, and entrenched themselves at Cabrerizos, watching the French Division at Babila Fuente.

Marmont, extending his left along the forest, still menaced the L. of C. with Ciudad Rodrigo.

Information also reached Wellington that 2000 horse, and 20 guns, under Chauvel, had reached Pollos from Caffarelli's Army. [Despatches, 24th July to Earl Bathurst.] Napier, Vol. IV., Book XVIII., ch. 3.

This rendered a final retreat on Portugal necessary, 'unless circumstances permitted Wellington to attack on the 22nd,' or, as Napier says, 'unless the enemy should commit some flagrant error.'

THE SALAMANCA CAMPAIGN.

22ND JULY.

At daybreak, Marmont called in the Division from Babila Fuente, by the ford of Encinas.

He brought two Divisions from the forest, and occupied Calvarisa de Ariba. He also took possession of the wooded height of Nuestra Señora de la Pena.

About 8 a.m., according to Jones, or noon, according to Alison, a French column seized the Outer Arapiles. This indicated the intention of the French to force the Allies back.

The Allies seized the other Arapiles, and a detachment from the 7th Division won back part of La Pena. General Packenham's Division with the Cavalry was brought across the Tormes, and posted near Aldea Tejada in support of the new right of the line. The Allied front had now changed. The new right was near Aldea Tejada, the left was near the English Arapiles, where the right had previously rested.

Marmont tried to hasten the supposed retreat of the Allies by a series of manœuvres. At 2 p.m. he extended rapidly to his left with a force little superior to the Allies, acting on the arc of a circle of one-third greater extent than their line.

In this movement, Thomières' Division, forming the left, became separated from the centre.

Then Wellington seized the opportunity, and launched his historic counterstroke.

[The above is only an outline of the events of the day. Much of this will be repeated in giving the detailed account of the battle.]

Marmont's policy was to keep close touch, but not to force on **Notes.** a battle unless the chances were distinctly in his favour. It appears that the Army of the Centre moved on the 21st, but the letter announcing this only reached Marmont on the 23rd.

Jealousy of the other Marshals, and a false estimate of Wellington's character, are said to have contributed to his precipitation.

CHAPTER V.

THE BATTLE OF SALAMANCA. JULY 22ND, 1812.

In considering the battle itself there are two difficulties: first, to reconcile the various accounts; secondly, to obtain a sufficiently clear map.

Preliminary Observations.

(1) Authorities.

With regard to the first point, there are:—

(1) Wellington's Despatches, Vol. IX., letters of 24th July to Earl Bathurst; and 25th, to Sir T. Graham. These are clear and to the point, and have the merit of being absolutely trustworthy; but they deal with one side only.

(2) Marmont's letter (quoted in Supplementary Despatches, Vol. XIV., p. 81). This is a good account from the French point of view, but takes the form of an 'apologia,' and therefore the facts are bound to be 'twisted' to a certain extent. All the blame for the defeat is thrown on a subordinate.

It is wonderful, however, that such a clear despatch was written whilst Marmont was suffering from so severe a wound.

There are also Marmont's Mémoires, which contain a fuller account of the battle, and give, besides the letter referred to above, another letter, dated 19th November, in answer to Napoleon's reproaches. In these Mémoires, and in the second letter, Marmont is even more outspoken in throwing the blame on his subordinate.

(3) Napier's and Thiers' accounts are exhaustive, and enter into eulogistic detail. They differ in some important points. There is also in the British Museum a translation of Napier, by Col. Dumas and other officers of the French General Staff. This contains notes and corrections, and in some particulars the text of the

27

translation differs from the original. This will be referred to in the Appendix.

(4) Alison, Gleig, and Jones give shorter accounts, and perhaps a clearer general idea of the battle.

(5) Kausler gives an extremely clear account of the dispositions; but, if his account were read without reference to other accounts, one would go away with the idea that it was a deliberately drawn up battle, and one would miss all idea of the gap in the French line, and of Wellington's great counterstroke.

(6) Maxwell's account is pleasant reading, but is a shorter and more general account of the battle.

(7) Capt. Lewis Butler gives an excellent account of the battle.

With regard to the second point, nearly all the maps suffer (2) **Maps.** from one great fault. They do not face North, nor indeed do they obey the rule of facing from one's own position to that of the enemy. In a battle so mixed up with the previous strategy, this is very confusing.

The maps in the pocket at the end of this book are chiefly based on a map prepared by Major Mitchell shortly after the battle, but have been made to face North, so as to compare more readily with the strategical maps.

STATE OF THE ALLIED FORCES.

(Wellington's Sup. Despatches, Vol. XIV., p. 62.)

INFANTRY.

1ST DIVISION—
Maj.-Gen. H. Campbell ... ...
{ Col. Hon. T. Fermor
Maj.-Gen. Wheatley
Maj.-Gen. Baron Low, K.G.L. }

3RD DIVISION—
Maj.-Gen. Hon. E. Packenham ... ...
{ Col. Wallace
Lieut.-Col. Campbell
Brig.-Gen. Power (Portuguese) }

4TH DIVISION—
Lt.-Gen. Hon. G. L. Cole ... ...
{ Maj.-Gen. W. Anson
Lieut.-Col. Ellis
Col. Stubbs (Portuguese) }

5TH DIVISION—
Lt.-Gen. Leith ... ...
{ Col. Greville
Maj.-Gen. Pringle
Brig.-Gen. Spry (Portuguese) }

6TH DIVISION—
Lt.-Gen. H. Clinton ... ...
{ Maj.-Gen. Hulse
Col. Hinch
Col. Douglas (Portuguese) }

7TH DIVISION—
Maj.-Gen. J. Hope ... ...
{ Maj.-Gen. de Bernewitz
Brig.-Gen. Conde de Rezende
(Portuguese) }

LIGHT DIVISION—
Maj.-Gen. Baron C. Alten ... ...
{ Col. Barnard
Maj.-Gen. Vandeleur
1st and 3rd Portuguese }

PORTUGUESE ... ...
{ Brig.-Gen. Pack
Brig.-Gen. Bradford }

CAVALRY.

Lt.-Gen. Sir S. Cotton ... ...
{ Maj.-Gen. Le Marchant
Mag.-Gen. G. Anson
Baron V. Alten
Baron Bock, K.G.L.
Brig.-Gen. d'Urban (Portuguese) }

RECAPITULATION OF THE NUMBERS PRESENT.

(Wellington's Sup. Despatches, Vol. XIV., p. 61.)

—	OFFICERS.	N.C.O.'s.	DRUMMERS.	R. AND F. PRESENT.
CAVALRY—British, Hanoverian, and Portuguese ...	211	248	46	3,986
INFANTRY—Ditto	2,030	2,220	954	39,986
SPANIARDS { Cavalry	...	..	...	500
{ Infantry	...	...	...	3,000
Present at Salamanca, not including Artillery and Engineers, whose state is mixed up with that of the Artillery and Engineers with Hill in Estremadura ...	2,241	2,472	1,000	47,466

ARTILLERY PRESENT :—

	GUNS.	HOWITZERS.	TOTAL.	TOTAL ORDNANCE.
3 Troops R.H.A.	15	3	18	
5 Brigades Royal and K.G.L. Artillery	25	5	30	} 48

Also 12 Spanish and Portuguese Guns, of which no state is given.

The Heavy Brigade of Artillery, 3 18-Pr. and 5 5½-in. Howitzers, arrived at the end of the battle, but were not in action.

THE SALAMANCA CAMPAIGN.

The 'Ordre de Bataille' of the two sides will first be given. That of the Allies is as follows. For details, *see page opposite.*

1st Division	...	...	...	Campbell *
3rd ,,	...	...	...	Packenham
4th ,,	...	...	...	Cole
5th ,,	...	...	...	Leith
6th ,,	...	...	...	Clinton
7th ,,	...	...	...	Hope
Light ,,	...	...	...	C. Alten
Portuguese Brigade	...	...	...	Pack
,, ,,	...	...	...	Bradford
Spanish ,,	...	...	...	Don Carlos d'Espagna

British Cavalry { Le Marchant ... ... }
{ Anson ... }
Hanoverian Cavalry, Bock ... } Stapleton Cotton
Portuguese Cavalry Bde., d'Urban ... }
(joined on July 17th)

The French 'Ordre de Bataille' is harder to obtain. Marmont's letter to Napoleon (Sup. Despatches, Vol. XIV., p. 81) gives the numbers of the Divisions, and also mentions some names of the Generals. From several books, including a French book† published in 1820, it would appear that Thomières commanded the 5th Division. But the following state is given in Dumas' translation of Napier, which is quoted in Sup. Despatches, Vol. XIV., p. 60 :—

1st Division	...	...	...	Foy
2nd ,,	...	...	...	Clausel
3rd ,,	...	...	...	Ferey
4th ,,	...	...	...	Sarrut
5th ,,	...	...	...	Maucune
6th ,,	...	...	...	Brennier
7th ,,	...	...	...	Thomières
8th ,,	...	...	...	Bonnet
Light Cavalry	...	...	...	Curto and Boyer

Making a total of about 42,000 present at the battle. Also 60 guns and 14 mortars.

---

* Kausler shows Paget commanding the 1st Division.

† 'Victoires, conquêtes, desastres, revers et guerres civiles des Français de 1792 à 1815, par une société de militaires et gens de lettres.'

THE SALAMANCA CAMPAIGN.

It is almost impossible to give an accurate account from a Note on historical accuracy. purely historical point of view of Marmont's real dispositions on the 22nd. All the accounts differ in the names of the Divisions and their relative positions on the field of battle.

Extracts from the different accounts, and a discussion as to the points of difference, will be given in the Appendix.

For the sake of continuity the narrative will be carried on here, giving the names of the Divisions as correctly as possible. From the point of view of the military student who is endeavouring to deduce the lessons of the campaign, such questions as whether Thomières or Maucune commanded the leading Division, or whether it was Clausel's or Brennier's Division that followed, are matters of very minor importance.

On the morning of the 22nd, Marmont called in his Division Morning of July 22nd. from Babila Fuente by the ford of Encinas, and in the meantime occupied the high ground about Calvarisa de Ariba, which had only been held by outposts on the previous night.

The British Light Cavalry followed, and watched the move from the heights of Nuestra Señora de la Pena.

About 8 a.m. a French column of Light Infantry (Bonnet's) 8 a.m. seized the Southern Arapiles, and mounted guns on it.

The British anticipated them by a few moments in seizing the Northern Arapiles with troops from the right wing and some guns.

At the same time, the 4th Division (Cole's), changing front, deployed to the right of this crest.

The seizure of the Arapiles by the French rendered a retreat by daylight difficult for the Allies, as Marmont could take any such movement in flank. Marmont explains that his object in seizing the Arapiles was to use it as a pivot of manœuvre round which he could work his way to the Allies' Line of Communication, and he protests that he had no intention of forcing on a battle.

In any case his project was not fully developed. The troops coming from Babila Fuente were several miles behind in the forest.

30

THE SALAMANCA CAMPAIGN.

According to Napier, he had only two Divisions up, and the occupation of Calvarisa de Ariba and Nuestra Señora de la Pena were
daring strokes to cover the concentration of his Army; but, according to Marmont's own account, his Army was already in mass
at the head of the woods.

Wellington, who had previously been doubtful as to which **Wellington's preliminary dispositions.**
bank of the Tormes Marmont intended to operate on, now con-
sidered that on the whole he intended to operate on the left bank.
He accordingly made the following dispositions:—He extended
the right of the Army, 'en potence,' by occupying the height
behind the Arapiles village with the 4th Division (Cole), less one
regiment, which remained on the Arapiles, and occupied that village
with the Light Companies of the Guards (1st Division). The
3rd Division (Packenham), with D'Urban's Cavalry, came from
Cabrerizos *via* Salamanca towards Aldea Tejada, where it was
ambushed between this village and the village of La Pinilla.
They were thus able to command the main road to Ciudad
Rodrigo.

The Dragoon Brigade covered the left wing near Pelabravo,
and the other Divisions moved more to the right as the enemy's
intentions became clearer.

The 1st Division, less the Light Companies of the Guards, and
the Light Division, were brought up to face the enemy's force on
Calvarisa; the 5th and 6th Divisions were massed on the slopes
of the Arapiles. The interval between the 3rd and 4th Divisions
was filled by a simple countermarch of Bradford's Portuguese Infantry, Don Carlos d'Espagna's Spanish Infantry, and the British
Cavalry, all massed near the village of Las Torres.

Thus the whole army changed front. The right became the
left, and the new right was pushed towards Aldea Tejada.

About 12 noon (or according to Marmont about 10 a.m.), **12 noon. Marmont's dispositions.**
Marmont, fearing that his position on the Arapiles would induce
Wellington to attack in force, brought up the 1st Division (Foy's),
and the 3rd Division (Ferey's), placing the former on the wooded

height between the Arapiles and N. S. de la Pena, and the latter, in support, further back on the Calvarisa de Ariba ridge.

Meantime the British baggage and commissariat wagons had been ordered to the rear. Their dust led Marmont to believe that a general retreat was in preparation. Fearing that the Allies would get out of his reach before his forces were fully concentrated, at 2 p.m. he took his resolution.　**2 p.m.**

He sent Maucune with two Divisions, covered by fifty guns, to the left to occupy the large plateau in front of that occupied by the Artillery. Thomières' Division was apparently the leading Division, and for this reason most of the accounts say that Thomières' was pushed to the left. It is probable, however, that Maucune was the senior of the Divisional Commanders on the left, and, for this reason, Marmont throws the blame on him. (For full discussion on this point see the Appendix.)

At the same time the march of the other French Divisions towards the centre was hastened, so as to fall with the rest of the Army on the flank of the British as they defiled past the French Arapiles. This was held by part of the 8th Division (Bonnet).

The 1st Division (Foy), on the summit of the Calvarisa de Ariba heights closed the right.

Thomières' Division reached the Peak of Miranda. Meantime the village of Arapiles was fiercely attacked, according to Napier, by part of Bonnet's Division; according to Thiers, by Maucune's Division (*vide* Appendix). The French, however, were quickly driven out of the greater part of the village, but a fierce struggle was maintained.

There now occurred a gap between the leading Divisions on the left and the centre of the French line. Whether this was **Gap in the French line.** caused by Thomières' and the succeeding divisions advancing too rapidly, or whether it was caused, as suggested by Thiers, by Maucune taking on himself to attack the centre of the Allied line, or whether it was caused by faulty dispositions on Marmont's part in sending on his left before his other divisions were concentrated, will be discussed later.

THE SALAMANCA CAMPAIGN.

On seeing the gap in Marmont's line, Wellington made rapid dispositions as follows :—

LEFT ...
- Two Dragoon Brigades (Bock and V. Alten) } to remain near Pelabravo.
- Light Division (C. Alten) — to deploy on left, behind Arapiles.
- 1st Division (Campbell) ... { detachments of Guards to occupy Arapiles village. rest to deploy in columns behind the Arapiles.
- Portuguese Brigade (Pack) — behind the Arapiles.

These were disposed in deep masses, as a Reserve, on the high ground behind the Northern Arapiles.

CENTRE ...
- 4th Division (Cole) ... } moved from left to centre, and deployed in two lines, forming the ' 1st line' (less Det. 4th Div. on Arapiles)
- 5th Division (Leith) ... }
- 6th Division (Clinton) ... } in 2nd line, as reserve, behind centre, formed in column.
- 7th Division (Hope) ... }
- Anson's Cavalry ... ... — flanking the 2nd line of the Centre.

These were intended for attack on Centre.

CONNECTING TROOPS ...
- Portuguese Brigade (Bradford) ... ...
- Spanish Brigade (Don Carlos) ... ... } to establish communication with the 3rd Division.
- Brigade British Heavy Cavalry (Le Marchant) ...

(Anson's and Le Marchant's Brigades were under Sir Stapleton Cotton.)

RIGHT ...
- 3rd Division (Packenham)
- Portuguese Cavalry Brigade) d'Urban) ... ... } near Aldea Tejada.
- Two Squadrons Heavy Cavalry (Hervey) ... ...

The Right, together with the Heavy Cavalry, was ordered to turn the enemy's left by the narrow valley of the Zerguen brook.

The Centre was ordered to attack as soon as the flank attack became developed.

Pack was ordered to attack the Southern Arapiles as soon as the flank of the 4th Division drew level with it, so as to prevent the flank of that Division from being exposed.

THE SALAMANCA CAMPAIGN.

These movements occupied till about 4 p.m. Marmont, from the French Arapiles, seeing the concentration on the British right, ordered the 3rd Division (Ferey) and the 4th Division (Sarrut) to emerge from the forest, so that he might dispose of them as required for the support of the left, now widely separated.

The intervening gap was imperfectly filled by the 2nd Division (Clausel) and the 5th Division (Maucune), who were separated both from the Centre and from the extreme left.

At this time Marmont only saw the British Centre advancing under heavy fire, the 3rd Division being hidden from him by the shape of the ground. He still had hopes of victory till the 3rd Division came into view, crossing Thomières' path. While hastening to this dangerous point he was severely wounded, was **Change of** succeeded by Bonnet, who had to be summoned from the right, **command on** and who was immediately disabled, and then by Clausel. **the French side.**

Thus there were three Commanders in succession in a very short space of time. This added to the confusion.

About 5 p.m. (Napier and Alison ; Kausler says 4 p.m.) the 3rd **5 p.m.** Division attacked, covered by its own guns and by two batteries **British right attack.** on the Western heights, and flanked on the right by d'Urban's and Hervey's Cavalry, and on the left by the British Cavalry.

They moved at right angles across Thomières' line of advance at the foot of the Peak of Miranda.

D'Urban's Portuguese Cavalry, supported by Hervey's British Dragoons, turned the French Left, and got in their rear.

At the same time Thomières' Right was menaced by the 5th Division (Leith). Thomières was killed, and his Division was forced back on Maucune, with the loss of 3000 prisoners.

About the same time— **British right centre.**

Bradford's Brigade ... 5th Division (Leith) ... 4th Division (Cole) ... followed in column in 2nd line by 7th Division (Hope) ... 6th Division (Clinton) ...	advanced in echelon from the right to attack parts of the French Left and Centre, composed of Clausel's Division and remnants of Thomières' and Maucune's.

THE SALAMANCA CAMPAIGN.

These were flanked on the right by Le Marchant's Heavy Dragoons and Anson's Light Cavalry, led by Sir Stapleton Cotton.

The interval between the 3rd Division on the right and 5th Division in the centre was suddenly filled by the Cavalry under Sir Stapleton Cotton, who charged right through the French Left and made over 2000 prisoners. **Cavalry charge.**

In this charge Le Marchant was killed.

The French Cavalry were driven from the field, and the French Divisions on the left no longer remained a formed body.

Anson's Light Cavalry, who had suffered little in the charge, joined hands with d'Urban's Cavalry, and with the 3rd and 5th Divisions formed one line more than a mile in front of the point from which Packenham had started.

Clausel made a great effort to save the day. He drew the 3rd Division (Ferey) from Calvarisa and placed it behind Bonnet. and joined with it the Light Cavalry, Boyer's Dragoons, and Brennier's and Sarrut's Divisions, so long expected from the forest. **French rally.**

Meantime Pack's attack on the Southern Arapiles had failed, and had been driven back. **British left centre.**

The 4th Division, advancing with the 5th Division, thereby had its left uncovered, and was attacked in flank by three Battalions of Bonnet's Division and by a Brigade of French Cavalry, and also by 1200 fresh troops from the reverse slopes of the Arapiles. **Local counterstroke by the French.**

Ferey pressed the front of the 4th Division, Brennier the first line of the 5th Division, and Boyer's Dragoons joined in.

The 4th and 5th Divisions were driven back. Beresford, who was on the spot, brought up a brigade from the second line of the 5th Division, made it change front to the left, and checked the advance of the enemy to some extent, but was himself badly wounded. **Beresford and Wellington bring up the reserves and restore the fight.**

35

THE SALAMANCA CAMPAIGN.

This was the crisis of the battle, and, as Napier says, 'Victory was for the General who had the strongest reserves in hand.'

Wellington brought up the 6th Division (Clinton), who by a gallant charge restored the fight.

The French Army fell back everywhere to a strong second position along the edge of the wood from N. S. de Otrero to the road to Alba de Tormes, behind the Ariba streamlet.

Meantime the Light Division, supported by the 1st Division **Left.** (Campbell), had forced the enemy's right wing under Foy to give way. Wellington directed the 1st Division to cut Foy off from the rest of the Army, which would have made it impossible, according to Napier, for the French Army to escape. But this was not carried out.

Clausel was able, therefore, to use Foy's Division and parts of **French** Bonnet's Division, which had come down from the Southern **rearguard.** Arapiles, added to the remnants of Maucune's command, to cover the retreat.

The former covered the roads to the fords of Huerta and Encinas ; the latter, reinforced by 15 guns, covered the roads to Alba de Tormes.

The rest of the French Army, retiring in disorder before the—

> 3rd Division (Packenham)
> 5th Division (Leith)
> 6th Division (Clinton),

took refuge behind the rearguard.

Wellington attacked the rearguards as follows :— **Wellington's dispositions.**

> Light Division (C. Alten) in two lines, ⎫
>   flanked by Dragoons, and supported by ⎬ against Foy, *i.e.,*
>   the 1st Division (Campbell) in column ⎭   French right.
>   and part of the 4th Division (Cole)

> Two Brigades 4th Division   ...   ... ⎫
> 6th Division (Clinton) ...   . ⎪ against Maucune,
> 3rd Division (Packenham)   ...   ... ⎬ *i.e.,* the rearguard
> 7th Division (Hope) ⎱   ⎪ on the Alba road.
> Spaniards   ⎰ in reserve   ... ⎭

THE SALAMANCA CAMPAIGN.

Foy fell back, contesting every inch of ground, especially the stream running from the wood into the Tormes. At one time, when part of the 4th Division had penetrated between him and Maucune, it seemed impossible that he should get away, but under cover of heavy musketry fire and a threatened Cavalry charge he succeeded in escaping into the woods.

Maucune's troops formed the last rearguard, and he commanded them with great skill and courage. When at last the 6th and 3rd Divisions reached the summit of the crest just as darkness was setting in, Maucune, having accomplished his task, retired into the woods.

Meantime, Wellington, in person, with the leading Regiment **Pursuit.** of the Light Division, was making straight across the fields for Huerta and the fords of the Tormes, believing that the Spaniards were still holding the Castle of Alba de Tormes.

This had, however, been evacuated by the Spanish Colonel in command, and his chief, Don Carlos d'Espagna, had not informed Wellington of the fact.

The French, who were aware of this, escaped by this passage **Escape of** without further molestation. Thus the full fruits of the victory **the French.** were lost, much to Wellington's discontent.

Next day, Wellington continued the pursuit. A rearguard **Continued** action was fought at La Serna, in which Bock's German Cavalry **pursuit.** made some historic charges.

The French reached Flores de Avila, forty miles from the battlefield, the night after the battle, and continued their retreat to the Douro.

Wellington pursued as far as Valladolid, where his force had to break into two portions, one to pursue the army under Clausel, the other to move against the King.

As with the numbers engaged, so with the losses; accounts **Losses.** vary.

The return in Wellington's despatches is as follows:—

THE SALAMANCA CAMPAIGN.

Return of Killed, Wounded, and Missing of the Allied Army under the command of General the Earl of Wellington, K.B., in the battle near Salamanca, on the 22nd June, 1812:—

	Officers.	Sergeants.	Rank and File.	Total.	British.	Portuguese.	Spanish.
Killed	41	28	625	694	388	304	2
Wounded	252	178	3,840	4,270	2,714	1,552	4
Missing	1	1	254	256	74	182	

The numbers given by Kausler are very similar in the totals, but give a smaller proportion of Officers killed and wounded.

Kausler describes the French losses as 'unknown, probably treble; the prisoners alone include 1 General, 186 Officers, 7,000 men, 11 guns, 2 eagles, 11 standards.'

The French losses, given by the Imperial Rolls, between 10th July and 10th August, including the battle of Salamanca, are as follows:—

	Killed or Taken.	Wounded.	Missing.
Officers	162	232	0
Men	3.867	7,529	645
Total	4,029	7,761	645

Total losses:—Officers and Men 12,435
Horses 1,190
Guns 12
Eagles 2

The Allies lost 1 General killed (Le Marchant), and 5 Generals wounded.

The French lost 2 Generals killed (Thomières and Ferey) and 4 Generals wounded (Marmont, Bonnet, Clausel, Maucune).

38

CHAPTER VI.

NOTES—DISCUSSION OF CRITICISMS—LESSONS AND POINTS TO BE THOUGHT OUT.

THERE are so many lessons to be learnt that it is only possible to mention a few of them, and these very briefly. Some of these, deduced from the earlier events, have already been mentioned on p. 3.

Besides the lessons to be learnt, we must also consider criticisms that have been made by various authorities, and the discrepancies in historical accounts.

These will be mixed up together, and not separated into classes, so as to take them in the same order as the narrative.

1. **Secrecy and mystification in War.**—Note the precaution Wellington took to mislead the enemy before marching to the siege of Badajos. *Cp.* Stonewall Jackson.

2. **The importance of time.**—Wellington, having mystified the enemy, commenced the siege of Badajos before he was fully ready, and finally assaulted it, at the risk of great loss, so as to carry out his plans before Soult could interfere.

3. **The effect of the Lines. of Torres Vedras.**—Not only their immediate effect in checking the French, but also their moral effect, in deterring Napoleon (according to Jones) from coming to Spain in person, and from risking prestige by being baffled, as Massena had been.

4. **Jealousy between Commanders.**—Note Marmont's delay in carrying out Napoleon's orders to advance into Beira, causing, according to Napoleon, by his vanity and jealousy, the loss of Badajos. This 'jealousy between Commanders' comes out repeatedly in the remainder of this campaign, and was the main cause of the undoing of the French in the Peninsula.

Caffarelli and Soult did not help Marmont as they had been ordered to do.

THE SALAMANCA CAMPAIGN.

Marmont, when he had outmanœuvred Wellington, made the fatal mistake which lost him the battle of Salamanca, through his anxiety to triumph before Joseph could come on the scene and share his laurels.

To descend lower, Maucune (or Thomières) pushed on at Salamanca in disobedience to Marmont's commands, and is accused by Marmont, in his letter to Napoleon, of always being a thorn in his side owing to his jealousy, which led to insubordination.

This brings us to another point :—

5. **Insubordination.**—Soult and Caffarelli showed it to Joseph. Drouet showed it to Soult. Maucune showed it to Marmont. There are innumerable instances of jealousy and insubordination all through the Peninsular campaign, and they will not be especially noted again in considering the narrative.

Other lessons, however, arise negatively from these :—

6. **The effect of one supreme head.**—Wellington as compared with the crowd of French Marshals.

7. **The value of a subordinate,** who is so in act as well as in name, and who is content to efface himself in working towards the common end. Hill is a notable instance, but the same may be said of nearly all of Wellington's Divisional and detached Generals.

8. **The effect of politics on Strategy.**—Wellington was prevented from operating against Soult in the South, owing to the action of the Spanish and Portuguese Governments in not carrying out their promises with regard to Almeida and Ciudad Rodrigo (p. 4). There are many other instances, including the failure of Sir W. Bentinck to make the promised diversion on the East Coast of Spain, and the action of the Home Government in diverting supplies and money which were intended for Wellington.

9. **Scattered versus concentrated forces, or Exterior versus Interior lines.**—The French Armies were scattered all over Spain, while Wellington was concentrated at a point from which he could strike them in detail. Here we see the *effect* of scattered versus concentrated forces, but we must remember that

40

the French were engaged in a war of conquest, and that it was almost impossible for them to be otherwise than scattered. We may compare what our position in South Africa in 1901 would have been supposing some European Power had placed a concentrated Army in the centre of the country while we were scattered over Cape Colony, Orange River Colony, and the Transvaal.

10. **Influence of Fortresses, Sea Base, etc.**—Wellington's position also gave him the advantage of the three fortresses of Almeida, Ciudad Rodrigo, and Badajos as pivots of manœuvre, of the lines of Torres Vedras on which he could fall back, of sea base, of water carriage, etc.

11. **Effect of Lines of Communication.**—Both Wellington and Napoleon looked on the line of communication from Bayonne as vital to the French Armies. Therefore, when Wellington had to decide whether to attack Marmont in the North or Joseph and Jourdan in the Centre, he chose the former, foreseeing what a great effect on the rest of Spain a victory in this quarter would have. His letter of May 26th, 1812, to Lord Liverpool is a model of an appreciation of the situation. Many people would have attached undue weight to the effect of capturing the capital and defeating the King.

Later on we see the great example of the maxim that the Army whose line of communications is most immediately threatened must conform to the movements of the adversary. Marmont, moving to Toro on July 15th–16th, threatened Wellington's communications, but also exposed his own. Marmont moving back to Wellington's right not only threatened Wellington's communications but also covered his own, and made secure his junction with the Army of the Centre; and Wellington had to conform to his movements.

12. **Careful preliminary preparations** (step by step).
    (1) Capture of the three fortresses.
    (2) Cutting enemy's shortest line of intercommunication (Almarez).

(3) Improving his own intercommunications (bridge of Alcantara).

(4) Preparation of Tagus waterway.

(5) Preparation of alternative bases, Guadiana and Agueda. Cp. Austerlitz.

13. **Soult's Plan.**—Here we see the effect that can be created by partisans, and the effect of strongholds. These caused Soult to lose the initiative.

We may also note that partisans decrease very much in value when they become large, unwieldy bodies. The officers are not trained and the men are not sufficiently disciplined to cope with regular troops. The question of supply becomes a difficult one. They can no longer appear and disappear, assemble and disperse, in the same bewildering fashion. We notice that these large bodies of partisans did not cause the French the same amount of anxiety as they did previously. They were more easily located.

14. **Separate to live, concentrate to fight.**—We see Marmont trying to imitate Napoleon's principle (cp. the Austerlitz campaign). Marmont, however, had to fall back to effect his concentration, and, if it had not been for the delay caused by the Salamanca Forts, he would have found his concentration still more difficult.

15. **Why did not Wellington attack Marmont on the 21st, and again on the 24th?**

Wellington has been freely criticised for not attacking on these dates, on the first of which, at all events, Marmont was far inferior in numbers to him. Even Napier joins in criticising Wellington's action (Vol. IV., pp. 240–242). Wellington himself (Despatches to Earl of Liverpool, June 25th, 1812, Vol. IX.) admits that between June 20th and 22nd he had a favourable opportunity for attacking, but he gives the following reasons for not availing himself of it :—

(1) Marmont appeared to be intending to attack. Wellington considered it to be more advantageous to be

42

attacked than to attack himself. The loss, also, would
be less.

(2) Some of the troops were engaged in the siege of the forts,
and though the Allies had a superiority in numbers, it
was not sufficient to ensure a decisive result. The loss
of men would be unnecessary.

(3) In the case of failure, the passage of the Tormes would
have been difficult, as the enemy still held the forts
which commanded the bridge at Salamanca.

In (1) we notice Wellington's favourite tactics. He always
preferred to commence on the defensive.

In (1) and (2) we notice how careful he was to avoid unnecessary loss; yet, when an important object was in view, as at
Badajos, he was prepared to make any sacrifice.

In (2) and (3) we notice how Wellington considered the
question from all points of view. Success, unless decisive, was not
sufficient. Failure was possible. If failure should occur the
means of retirement had to be considered. Cp. Napoleon before
Austerlitz.

The same explanation would apply to the 24th, with the
addition that in the meantime Marmont had been strongly
reinforced.

**16. Why did Wellington, who had expressed his inten-
tion of bringing Marmont to battle, stop on reaching the
Douro ?**

Wellington gives the answer to this in Despatches to Earl
Bathurst of July 7th and July 14th.

After mentioning the strength of the enemy's position, the
paucity of the fords, the reinforcements to the enemy, he says:
' It is obvious we could not cross the river without sustaining
great loss, and could not fight a general action under circumstances of greater disadvantage than those which would attend
the attack of the enemy's position on the Douro. In truth, the
enemy's numbers are equal, if not superior, to ours; they have in

their position twice the amount of Artillery which we have, and we are superior in Cavalry alone, which arm, it is probable, could not be used in the attack we should have to make.'

He goes on to speak of the diversions he wished made from the North.

The truth is the critics have not realised the effect which the unexpected strength of the Salamanca Forts had on Wellington's plan of campaign. He came forward intending to meet and crush Marmont, but the strength of the forts, which he could not ignore, delayed him ten days. This delay made all the difference. It gave Marmont time to concentrate, to send for reinforcements, etc.

17. Why did Marmont, who had been falling back, suddenly assume the offensive?

The reasons for this are rather complicated.

    (1) Two letters were received from Joseph, saying that he considered Marmont strong enough to beat Wellington, whose Army consisted of 50,000 men, of whom only 18,000 were British.

    (2) He heard that no help was to be expected from Caffarelli or from Suchet, and that the former had been ordered to return to France.

    (3) He feared he would soon have to make detachments (a) to revictual Astorga (b) to contain the Army of Gallicia, 15,000 strong.

    (4) He feared that Hill with 12,000 men would join Wellington, and, at the same time, was convinced that Drouet and Soult would fail to contain Hill, and would fail to send the reinforcements which they had been ordered to send.

In addition, we must remember that Napoleon had in the Spring reproached Marmont very severely for his timorous and hesitating methods, by which he had failed to prevent the capture of Badajos.

The remaining points can only be touched on very briefly. and are put forward here as suggestions for subjects which the student of the campaign may think out and can elaborate for himself.

18. **Why had the Armies of Joseph and Soult** not taken advantage of the ten days' delay, caused by the siege of the forts, to come to Marmont's assistance? (See paragraphs 4 and 5.)

19. **Why did Marmont not continue his movement via Toro?** Critics have pointed out that it took him three days' hard marching to get to a point as near Wellington's communications as he had been on the night of the 15th–16th.

But on that night both armies would have been *equally* well situated for an attack on the enemy's communications, and *equally* unfavourably placed for an attack on their own. Defeat would have been ruin to either.

It is also said that if Napoleon had been in Marmont's place, he would have prepared a second line of communications to Benavente.

This would probably not have been an easy matter for Marmont to do, with the difficulty of obtaining supplies and with the Guerillas let loose on his flanks and rear.

Moreover, it would have meant giving up his hold on part of the centre of Spain, and, if defeated, being pushed back to the North-West corner. He was aware that the Army of Gallicia was on its way down to meet him, and could have combined with Wellington.

Finally, he would not have secured his connection with the King and Madrid.

Thus the disadvantages, even if he shifted his communications, would be many; and we may note that the great critic, Napoleon, does not criticise Marmont for not going on from Toro.

20. **Wellington's movements on the 18th July** are already commented on (p. 21).

THE SALAMANCA CAMPAIGN.

21. We should note throughout the manœuvring between Marmont and Wellington, and in the preliminary movements on the battlefield; (1) **the consummate knowledge of country,** and (2) **the power of handling troops which each displayed.**

They had both moved backwards and forwards over this country before, but in itself this would not have been enough. We know that Wellington's eye for country was phenomenal, and that he was always observing country he passed over with a view to the possibility of having to fight on it one day; yet Napier says, 'The French General was more perfectly acquainted with the ground, and moved his army with a wonderful facility.' (Vol. IV., p. 259.)

It was a case of Greek meeting Greek, and this is why these manœuvres are so interesting to study.

Then with regard to the handling of the troops: Wellington's brilliant tactics during the retirement on the 18th have already been noted, the movements from then to the 22nd are noteworthy, and the dispositions of Wellington during the preliminary operations of that day (described on p. 31) are deserving of the closest study.

The wonderful facility with which the change of front was made to meet the new situations, as Marmont's projects became clearer, is particularly interesting.

Again, we should note that though there were two faces to the position, at less than a right angle, the salient was made strong by the British Arapiles height, and by the village of Arapiles, and that the two forces were able to act in harmony at the close of the battle.

We should also note the expression 'flanked by cavalry.' There was no body on the field that day that had not an attendant body of cavalry in rear of one flank.

We should note the bringing up of the 3rd Division from Cabrerizos to a position of readiness, the way it was concealed

THE SALAMANCA CAMPAIGN.

from view, and the precautions taken to connect it with the main body.

We should note, and this applies especially to modern times, the clearness of the orders given to the various parts of the attack before it was launched (see p. 33). The timing of the various parts of this great counterstroke was one of its finest features.

We should note how the dispositions which placed the bulk of the Cavalry in the corner between the turning movement and frontal attack, brought about an ideal opportunity for the use of Cavalry on the battlefield.

The retention of the Reserves and their employment at the right moment should also be noted. Also that the left of the line was really a large Reserve, so placed that it was able to act on the enemy's strategic flank.

We talk much nowadays about the combination of the three arms, but in practice, in field-days, and in tactical schemes this combination is generally confined to two of the three arms, artillery and infantry, and the cavalry is forgotten, or hardly made use of at all. At Salamanca the reverse seems almost to have been the case. It is extraordinary how little mention is made of the guns in any account of the campaign, English or French. 'Thomières advanced covered by fifty guns;' 'Packenham attacked, covered by guns;' 'Wellington did not cross the Douro because the French were stronger in guns.' This is nearly all we hear of the guns, and it starts us on an interesting line of thought regarding the evolution of the three arms in the last hundred years.

22. **The Counterstroke.**—It has been asked, was this a prepared Counterstroke, in the sense that the Counterstroke at Austerlitz was prepared?

It hardly could be so. At Austerlitz Napoleon took up a carefully prepared position, with a carefully prepared line of retreat; tempted the enemy to attack him in a certain way, and launched his Counterstroke.

47

THE SALAMANCA CAMPAIGN.

Here the Allies had been racing for seven days to prevent
their communications being turned, had taken up one position after
another and been manœuvred out of them, and had been forced to
conform to the enemy's movements.

This can only be called a prepared Counterstroke in the sense
that Wellington's dispositions were such that he was ready for all
eventualities, and was ready to take advantage of any mistake made
by the enemy.

The enemy, by his undue extension, gave him the opportunity of bringing superior force to bear at the decisive point,
and he took it, launching three-fourths of his force in the
Counterstroke.

23. **Rearguard.**—The able way in which Clausel collected a
rearguard out of the remnants of his beaten Army, and the equally
able dispositions made by Wellington to drive in that rearguard,
should be considered, as also the advantage of fighting a rearguard action in front of a large wood.

24. **Pursuit.**—Wellington's pursuit after the victory has been
much criticised. Morris says, ' but Wellington could not follow up
the victory with the vigour and wonderful art of Napoleon,' com-
paring Salamanca with Austerlitz.

But it must be remembered that Austerlitz began at daybreak
and was over by noon, and that Salamanca did not begin till
nearly 4 p.m., and was not over till dark.

Secondly, that the majority of Napoleon's troops had been
stationary for several days before the fight, whereas at Salamanca
the Allies had been marching and fighting from the 16th to 22nd.

Thirdly, that the mental strain of those seven days must
have been very severe, not only on Wellington, but on all his
subordinate officers.

Fourthly, that Austerlitz was a somewhat one-sided fight
compared with Salamanca, and that there was no able General on
the defeated side to conduct the retreat. Moreover, that the
vanquished were composed of Allies, one of which had been

beaten and harassed before the battle, and the other had but little experience in war. Whereas at Salamanca Clausel was a very able commander, assisted by men like Maucune and Foy, and the men were French veterans.

Wellington instituted immediate pursuit, led it in person to a point at which he would have cut off the whole French army, if he had not been betrayed by a subordinate.

The pursuit was taken up next morning at daylight, and continued till Clausel was pushed across the Douro, and irrevocably separated from the Army of the Centre. Valladolid was occupied, and the pursuit divided into two portions, one portion pursuing Clausel up to Arlanza, the other moving against the King, and reaching Cuellar on the 1st August.

From Salamanca to Valladolid, via Arevalo and Olmedo, is 90 miles. Clausel was pushed over the Douro, at Valladolid, on July 29th. This means an average of 13 miles a day, with constant skirmishes and fighting.

WELLINGTON'S GENERAL ORDER TO THE TROOPS AFTER SALAMANCA.

TORDILLOS, 23RD JULY, 1812.

1. The Commander of the Forces returns his thanks to the General Officers, Officers and troops for their conduct in the action with the enemy on the 22nd inst., of which he will not fail to make to His Royal Highness the Prince Regent the favourable report that it deserves.

2. He trusts that the events of yesterday have impressed all with the conviction that military success depends upon troops obeying the orders which they receive, and preserving the order of their formation in action, and that upon no occasion they will allow themselves to depart from it for one moment.

WELLINGTON.

APPENDIX.

EXTRACTS from the accounts of Napier, Alison, Marmont, and Thiers, are given below for comparison.

It must be remembered that Marmont is making the best of a bad defeat, and is on his defence, especially in his letter of November 19th, in answer to Napoleon's reproaches and categorical questions. In his Mémoires he throws the blame on Maucune much more openly than he does in his two official letters.

Thiers' account of the movements of the French Divisions is very clear and detailed, and follows Marmont very closely; but even between these two there are considerable discrepancies. On the face of it these French writers ought to be better informed of the dispositions of the French Divisions than the English writers, and, if they agreed, it would be natural to adopt Thiers' description of the French movements, and Wellington's and Napier's of the English.

In the Wellington Despatches, which give clearly our own movements, no mention is made of the names of the opposing Divisions.

Napier's account is on the whole the clearest and most consistent, and I should be inclined to follow it as correct, if it were not for the fact that Marmont ought to be the best authority for the orders issued to his Divisions.

The main points of difference between the accounts are as follows:—

1. Napier says: 'On the morning of 22nd, Marmont brought Bonnet's and Maucune's Divisions from the forest and occupied Calvarisa de Ariba.' Later on he says, 'Foy's and Ferey's Divisions were brought up in support.' **Occupation of Calvarisa de Ariba.**

Marmont says: 'Foy and Ferey were ordered to occupy Calvarisa Ariba;' but he also says that 'Maucune's Division (5th) was with the 2nd, 4th, and 6th, in mass at the head of the woods.'

2. Napier also says: 'Marmont had only two Divisions up, and the occupation of Calvarisa Ariba and Nostra Senora de la Pena were daring strokes to cover the concentration of his army.'

Marmont, in his Mémoires, describes his 'remaining six Divisions at the head of the wood in two lines,' and in his letter of 31st July shows them as all present at the head of the wood. (*Cp.* also 'Gleig,' and 'Victoires, Conquêtes, etc.')

51

APPENDIX.

Extension to the left. 3. The main difference between the accounts is as to what Divisions performed the extension to the left.

The difficulty as to whether it was Maucune or Thomières is, I think, easily overcome. Maucune was probably the Senior of the Divisional Generals on the left, but Thomières' Division was furthest to the left. Most writers only use the name Thomières. Marmont throws all the blame on Maucune; Napier speaks of Maucune all through, till the actual attack by Packenham is described. He then says: 'Packenham fell on Maucune's 1st Division under Thomières.' Dumas' translation of Napier mentions Thomières all through.

The greater difficulty is the name of the remaining Division of the left extension.

Alison, in his edition of 1850 and previous editions, says: 'Thomières' Division, followed by Clausel and Bonnet,' and describes Thomières and Clausel advancing too rapidly, and a chasm appearing between their Divisions and Bonnet's.

This account differs from all others, and I think may be dismissed.

But in his edition of 1860 he says: 'Thomières followed by Brennier and Maucune,' and adds a footnote at the end of the chapter explaining why he made this alteration.

Gleig places the Divisions in the same order, viz., Thomières, Brennier, Maucune.

Marmont says he ordered Maucune to the extreme left, Thomières in second line, Clausel to act as reserve, Brennier to hold the plateau at the head of the wood, *i.e.*, well to the rear. He goes on to say that Maucune extended without rhyme or reason. Thomières, instead of supporting, came level; and Clausel was still behind. He then ordered up Ferey and Sarrut from the wood.

Thiers says :—

Thomières...	...	...	extreme left.
Maucune ...	...	...⎫	
Sarrut	...	...⎬	centre.
Clausel	...	..	in reserve.
Brennier	...	...	in rear towards the baggage.

and goes on to say that 'Maucune, who commanded the Division of the centre furthest to the left, caused the gap by advancing against the Allied centre, while Thomières continued his course to the left.'

But Napier, who does not mention the 3rd Division of the left extension, describes Clausel later in the fight as making Sarrut's, Ferey's, and Brennier's

52

APPENDIX.

'unbroken Divisions' act as a mass on which 'the three Divisions under Maucune' might rally.

Marmont also says that, seeing the wide extension on the left, he ordered up Ferey and Sarrut.

From this I think we must deduce that Sarrut's Division was not one of the three.

Bonnet's Division is only mentioned in the earlier editions of Alison, and we know it was engaged at the Arapiles.

Ferey's and Foy's were engaged at Calvarisa de Ariba.

There now only remain Brennier's and Clausel's Divisions.

Brennier's Division is mentioned by Alison (1860) and Gleig as being the second Division on the left, but by all others it is mentioned as being in rear with the baggage, except in one place in Thiers' account, where it is mentioned as having hastened to the left to Thomières' assistance.

On the other hand, Clausel is described by Thiers as being still in rear, and not in position to support the left extension. Marmont, in his letter of July 31st, confirms this. Napier describes Clausel later in the fight as having just arrived from the forest.

There is this objection to Clausel's Division forming one of the three on the left, namely, that Clausel must have been senior to Maucune, as he subsequently took command of the Army, yet Napier speaks of the 'three Divisions under Maucune.'

A possible explanation is that when Clausel took command of the whole force his Division came under Maucune's command.

The version, therefore, which, I think, is the most consistent with the best accounts, may be briefly summed up as follows :—

Maucune, with two Divisions (as stated by Napier), *i.e.*, his own and Thomières', was pushed to the left. Foy and Ferey were on the right. Bonnet was in the centre, on the Arapiles. Clausel was in reserve, while Brennier was at the head of the wood in rear, and Sarrut had not yet come out of the woods.

This agrees with Marmont's orders.

About the time that Marmont was wounded, Clausel was coming up in support of Maucune; but on Clausel taking over command of the whole Army his Division passed under the command of Maucune. This accounts for Napier speaking of 'the three Divisions under Maucune.'

Marmont mentions calling up Ferey's and Sarrut's Divisions from the wood, and Thiers of Brennier hastening to the assistance of the left.

53

APPENDIX.

This would agree with Napier, who speaks of 'the unbroken Divisions of Sarrut, Brennier, and Ferey covering the retreat of the broken left.'

Captain Lewis Butler, in his excellent account of the battle, adopts, I find, a similar version to this.

Alison's footnote to his edition of 1860, however, shows that he went carefully into the evidence, and his version may be the correct one; but, pending further evidence, I have given in the text the version of which a short summary is given above.

EXTRACTS.

Napier.

On 21st, Marmont passed the Tormes between Alba and Huerta, then, moving by the valley of the Machacon, encamped behind Calvarisa Ariba at the edge of a forest, which extended from the river to that place . . . . lest the French, who had left a Division on the heights of Babila Fuente, should recross the Tormes in the night. . . . . But at daybreak (22nd) Marmont, who had called his troops from Babila Fuente by the ford of Encinas, brought *Bonnet's* and *Maucune's* Divisions from the forest, and occupied Calvarisa Ariba; he also took possession of the wooded height of N. S. de la Pena . . . . his troops coming from Babila Fuente were still in the forest several miles distant; he had only two Divisions up, and the occupation of Calvarisa and S. de la Pena were daring strokes to cover the concentration of his army . . . . about 12 o'clock Marmont hastily brought *Foy's* and *Ferey's* Divisions in *support*, placing the first with some guns on a wooded height between the Hermanitos and the S. de la Pena; the second, reinforced by Boyer's Dragoons, he posted behind Foy on the Calvarisa ridge. . . . . Although the Division from Babila Fuente had not yet come out of the forest, Marmont suddenly directed *Maucune with two Divisions*, covered by fifty guns and Light Cavalry, to move by their left and menace the Rodrigo road; designing, if his adversary moved in opposition, to fall on him by the village of Arapiles with *six divisions* and Boyer's Dragoons, leaving only one regiment Cavalry on Foy's right . . . . The Eastern side was held by the French, and their left, under Maucune, was moving along the Southern ridges, but there was a long interval between him and the troops about Hermanitos, and the Divisions destined to fill the gap were still in the forest. . . . . At this time *Bonnet's troops* carried the village of Arapiles . . . . when, by the rash advance of his left, his troops were separated into three parts, each at too great a distance to assist the other . . . . until he saw Packenham with the 3rd Division shoot like a meteor across *Maucune's path*. . . . . It was about

54

APPENDIX.

5 o'clock when Packenham fell on Maucune's *first Division under Thomières.*
. . . . Bonnet's Division had been repulsed from the Arapiles village . . . .
but the French still kept their menacing position at the Hermanito, for *Clausel's*
division *had arrived from the forest*, and the connection between the centre and
the left was in some measure restored. Two Divisions of Infantry and Boyer's
Dragoons were indeed still in march from Calvarisa . . . . and though Clausel's
own Division reinforced Maucune . . . . (Cavalry charge) . . . . the left was
thus entirely broken, the *three Divisions under Maucune* no longer existed as a
military body. . . . . Clausel drawing Ferey's Division from Calvarisa had placed
it in the centre behind Bonnet's troops, and at the same time had united there
the Light Cavalry, Boyer's Dragoons, and the two Divisions so long expected
from the forest. By this he offered a mass for the broken left to rally on, and
made *Sarrut's, Brennier's*, and *Ferey's* unbroken Divisions cover the line of
retreat, while another Division was in mass behind Marmont's, Hermanito and
Foy remained untouched on the right.

    1. Account of Salamanca in Marmont's Mémoires.   **Marmont.**

    2. Letter of 31st July in Marmont's Letters, also quoted in Supplementary
Despatches, Vol. XIV.

    3. Letter of November 19th to Ministre de la Guerre in answer to cate-
gorical questions by Napoleon.

    In 2 (official), and in 1, which is unofficial, and which amplifies 2,
Marmont says :—

1st Division	(Foy)	was ordered to occupy and defend Calvarisa de Ariba.
3rd ,,	(Ferey)	was ordered to support in 2nd line.
2nd ,,	(Clausel)	
4th ,,	(Sarrut)	were in mass at head of wood behind Arapiles
5th ,,	(Maucune)	position.
6th ,,	(Brennier)	
7th ,,	(Thomières)	held on the left of the wood a very steep knoll, with twenty guns.
Light Cavalry		on left, and in front of 7th.

Wellington reinforced his right, therefore Marmont had to reinforce his
left. In front of the plateau occupied by the Artillery there was another
large plateau. At 2 p.m. he ordered :—

    5th Division (Maucune) to take position on the extreme right of the
                           plateau, from which it could link its fire with
                           that from the Arapiles.

APPENDIX.

7th Division (Thomières) to place itself in the 2nd line to support the 5th.

2nd   „   (Clausel)   to hold itself in reserve behind.

6th   „   (Brennier)   to hold the plateau at the head of the wood, where there was still a large number of guns.

8th   „   (Bonnet)   to occupy an intermediate knoll between the plateau and the Arapiles.

. . . . At this moment Maucune told him the enemy was retreating, and asked leave to attack. He told Maucune to keep quiet. . . . . Then follow strictures on Maucune. Maucune took on himself to descend into the valley and to attack.

In 2, he adds :—

    (Maucune)   The 5th extended without rhyme or reason.

    (Thomières)   The 7th, instead of supporting, came level.

    (Clausel)   The 2nd was still in the rear.

    (Ferey and Sarrut) { He ordered the 3rd and 4th to emerge from the wood and come to the front, so that he might dispose of them as he wished.

    He was then wounded.

In 3, Marmont says he did not mean to fight. It was the enemy who attacked. Marmont wished to take a good defensive position at the head of the woods of Calvarisa de Ariba, and wait for reinforcements.

On 22nd it seemed indispensable to occupy the Calvarisa de Ariba heights with one Division, and also the Arapiles with one Regiment, supported by the rest of that Division. He kept the remaining six Divisions at the head of the wood in two lines.

He saw enemy moving to his right, and thought it necessary to occupy the large plateau in front. He therefore withdrew *three divisions* from the wood to occupy it. . . . The three Divisions, instead of placing themselves as ordered and keeping concentrated, spread out, one of them even going down off the plateau without rhyme or reason.

Alison.
[1850 and previous editions.]

Thomières' Division, covered by fifty guns, was pushed to the extreme left, to menace the C. R. road. He was followed by Clausel and Bonnet, while the march of all the French Divisions towards the centre was hastened, in order, with the remainder of the army, comprising four Divisions, to fall on the flank of the British as they defiled past the Arapiles.

. . . . Meanwhile, Thomieres' Division, followed by Clausel, advanced too rapidly . . . . and a chasm appeared between their Divisions and that of Bonnet,

56

APPENDIX.

which succeeded them and formed the nearest part of the centre. . . . . . Marmont ordered Clausel and Bonnet to move to his support. . . . . Thomières' Division, on the extreme left, was two leagues from their centre, and Clausel and Bonnet imperfectly filled the gap.

Thomières' Division, covered by fifty guns, was pushed to the extreme left **Alison.** to menace the C. R. road. He was followed by Brennier's and Maucune's. . . . [1860 edition.]

This height (Arapiles) was held by Bonnet, Foy on the summit of the plateau of Calvarisa de Ariba closing the right.

Meanwhile Thomières' Division, followed by Brennier's, advanced too rapidly, and a chasm appeared between their Divisions and that of Maucune, which succeeded them and formed the nearest part of the centre. . . . Marmont ordered Brennier and Maucune to move to his support. . . . . Thomières' Division on their extreme left was two leagues from their centre, and Brennier and Maucune imperfectly filled up the gap, being themselves separated by a distinct interval from the one and the other. . . . . Thomières' whole Division was thrown back utterly routed on Brennier's. . . . . Cole and Leith moved forward against part of the enemy's left and centre, composed of Brennier's Division, now united with Thomières' remains, and that of Maucune. . . . . . (Cavalry charge.) . . . . Leith and Cole had driven Maucune's troops back step by step on the broken remains of Brennier's and Thomières' Divisions. . . . . Clausel took command. . . . . his own men assailed the front of the 4th Division, Sarrut did the same to the 5th. . . . . Ferey was mortally wounded. (Note.— No mention is made of when Ferey came into action.) Then follows an account of the rearguard.

The footnote is as follows :—' In my former editions I had followed that brilliant and in general most accurate historian (Napier). An attentive examination and comparison, however, of the recent works, founded on official documents, of Belmas, Thiers, and Marmont, has convinced me that they were as stated in the text. Compare Marmont, IV., 133, 140, with Thiers, XV., 91, 98, and Belmas, I., 232, 234.

The Division of the Advanced Guard, under General Bonnet, threw itself **Gleig.** on one of the French Arapiles.

Foy's and Ferey's Divisions, supported by Boyer's Division of Dragoons, held the right, leaning on the plateau of Calvarisa, and covered by a wide ravine.

APPENDIX.

The Divisions of Clausel, Sarrut, Maucune, and Brennier were assembled *en masse* upon the centre in rear of the hill of the Arapiles, where Bonnet was posted.

On the left Thomières' Division, flanked by Curto's Division of Light Cavalry, occupied another plateau, which was defended by twenty pieces of cannon. . . . . .

Thomières' Division was directed, about two in the afternoon, to effect this object, in which it was supported by fifty guns, besides the light Cavalry of Curto and the Divisions of Maucune and Brennier. Nevertheless, these two latter Divisions were not yet in line when Thomières had already taken possession of the height in question (Miranda). . . . . . (Description of attack on Thomières.) While this was going on, the English troops debouched from the village of Arapiles, and cut to pieces a portion of Brennier's Division, which, after having imprudently engaged some troops at the entrance of the village, had halted to support them. They next overthrew Thomières' Division. . . . . finally driving back with the bayonet Maucune's Division.

Thiers.

Leaving his right under Foy at Calvarisa Ariba, and strengthening it with Ferey's Division, Marmont made his centre and left defile past this appui along the woods, against which he rested, and following the edge of the heights which he had occupied.

Bonnet's Division cleared the nearer Arapiles. This formed a strong pivot.

Marmont brought the rest of Divisions forward, left in front.

Thomières, forming his extreme left, advanced to threaten the English right.

Divisions of Sarrut and Maucune placed themselves in the centre, Clausel's Division in reserve, Brennier's Division in rear toward the baggage and artillery park.

. . . . Marmont, possessed of a fatal impatience, carried still further forward his left, composed of Thomières' Division, so much forward that it began to descend from the heights towards the 3rd Division (English). He brought his centre, composed of the Divisions of Maucune and Sarrut, nearer to the valley which separated us from the English, supported them by Clausel, and brought Brennier's Division nearer. . . . . Maucune, commanding the Division of the centre, which was furthest in front to the left, believing that the enemy was in full retreat, asked leave to attack, did not wait permission, but descended into the interval between the armies, and engaged against the English Divisions of the centre, those of Cole and Leith.

58

APPENDIX.

While Maucune committed this audacious mistake, Thomières on the left continued to advance. . . . .

Unfortunately, Clausel's Division . . . . was still in rear.

Marmont was wounded. While they went to look for Bonnet on the right near the Arapiles, ... Maucune drove back the English to the village of Arapiles, supported by Sarrut. . . . . Maucune had to give way, but Clausel arrived, took the place of Maucune's Division, and pushed back the English.

Lightning Source UK Ltd.
Milton Keynes UK
UKHW050955311018
331505UK00004B/28/P